W9-AOL-800

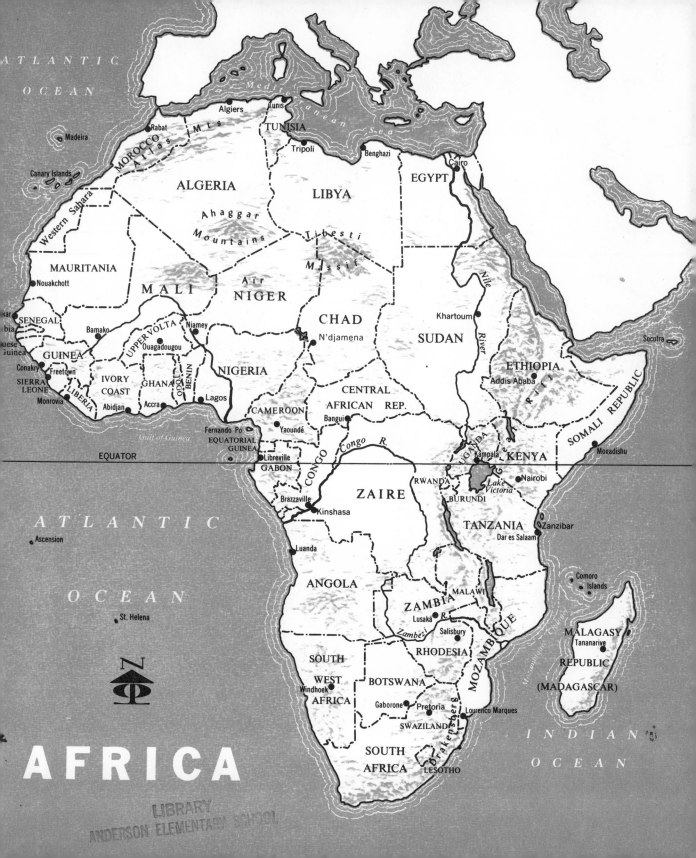

AFRICA

Enchantment of Africa

NIGERIA

by ALLAN CARPENTER

Consulting Editor
John N. Paden
Professor
Political Science Department
Northwestern University
Evanston, Illinois

 CHILDRENS PRESS, CHICAGO

THE ENCHANTMENT OF AFRICA

Available now: Algeria, Benin (Dahomey), Botswana, Burundi, Cameroon, Central African Republic, Chad, Congo (Brazzaville), Egypt, Equatorial Guinea, The Gambia, Gabon, Ghana, Guinea, Ivory Coast, Kenya, Lesotho, Liberia, Libya, Malagasy Republic (Madagascar), Malawi, Mali, Mauritania, Morocco, Niger, Nigeria, Rhodesia, Rwanda, Senegal, Sierra Leone, Sudan, Swaziland. Tanzania, Togo, Tunisia, Uganda, Upper Volta, Zaïre Republic (Congo Kinshasa), Zambia
Planned for the future: Equatorial Guinea, Ethiopia, Somalia, South Africa

ACKNOWLEDGMENTS

Embassy of the United States of America, Lagos; Federal Ministry of Information of Nigeria, Lagos

Cover: A street scene in Lagos, Allan Carpenter
Frontispiece: Women perform a traditional dance,
  Agency for International Development

Project Editor: Joan Downing
Assistant Editor: Elizabeth Rhein
Map Artist: Eugene Derdeyn

LIBRARY OF CONGRESS
CATALOGING IN PUBLICATION DATA

Carpenter, John Allan, 1917-
  Nigeria.
  (Enchantment of Africa)

  SUMMARY: Introduces the geography, history, government, economy, culture, and people of the largest coastal state of West Africa.
  1. Nigeria—Juvenile literature. [1. Nigeria]
I. Title.
DT515.C37   966.9'05   77-20793
ISBN 0-516-04579-2

Contents

A TRUE STORY TO SET THE SCENE 6
    Unity and Reconciliation

THE FACE OF THE LAND 9
    From Tropics to Desert—The Waters of Nigeria—Natural and
    Artificial—Climate

FOUR CHILDREN OF NIGERIA 16
    Flora of Jos—Yakubu of Lagos—Elizabeth of Owerri—Mohammed
    of Kano

NIGERIA YESTERDAY 31
    The Nok—Kanem-Borno—Hausa-Fulani—The Yoruba—European
    Beginnings—Slavery and Salvation—Exploring the Niger—The
    New Religion—British Rule—Leanings Toward Nationhood

NIGERIA TODAY 41
    Independence—Civil Strife—Yakubu Gowon—Overthrow—
    Government—Education

NATURAL TREASURES 50
    Mineral Riches—Field and Forest—Wildlife

THE PEOPLE LIVE IN NIGERIA 56
    Diverse Millions—Living Standards—Health and Welfare—Religion—
    Social Class—Marriage and Family—Sharo—Music—Art—
    Literature

THE PEOPLE WORK IN NIGERIA 69
    Farm and Forest—Manufacturing—Transportation and Communication

ENCHANTMENT OF NIGERIA 78
    A Fantastic Place—Lagos—Yorubaland and the South—Other-
    Worldly Jos—The Mysterious North—Dissimilarity and Unity

HANDY REFERENCE SECTION 91
    Instant Facts—Population—Economy—Agriculture—Legal Public
    Holidays—You Have a Date with History

INDEX 94

A True Story to Set the Scene

UNITY AND RECONCILIATION

On January 15, 1970, the world rejoiced at the official close of what American writer Carl Rowan called "one of the grimmest civil wars in history." As many as two million people had died as a result of this struggle. The central government had spent a billion dollars to win the war, and the wreckage of Nigeria's East Central State, renamed Biafra by supporters of the region's independence, totaled much more.

Whole cities, such as Onitsha and Owerri, lay in ruins. Much of the world had taken sides over the conflict, often with fierce bitterness.

When the war ended, most of the world expected the Biafrans who were responsible for the civil war would be executed or harshly treated and the rebellious region would be made to suffer for its actions. This is the kind of retribution that has happened time and time again throughout history.

Nigeria, however, was to be different. Its leader, Chief of State Yakubu "Jack" Gowon, had felt it would be disastrous if any part of Nigeria should break away permanently—especially its richest area and most powerful people.

So he had taken his government into war to keep the Ibo people of Biafra from breaking away.

But as soon as the war ended, General Gowon took far-reaching steps to prove to the Ibo people that they would not be

These blankets are part of a shipment of relief supplies that went to refugees of the Biafran civil war in East Central State.

treated as a conquered nation. There would be an official policy of "no victor and no vanquished."

A general amnesty for "all who were misled" into civil war was declared. A promise of no reprisals was made, and steps were taken to bring East Central State back into full partnership in the nation.

Anthony Asika, an Ibo who had remained loyal to the central government, became East Central State's governor. Eight of the eleven members of Asika's new cabinet had been on the side opposing the government.

Before a year had ended, more than 200,000 Ibo people had been restored to their old jobs. Some of the leaders of the rebellion were given important government posts. Vast quantities of food, medical care, clothing, and temporary shelter poured into East Central State to take care of the emergency needs of the people.

Then vast reconstruction efforts began, with the help of the government's 250,000-member army (black Africa's largest and most powerful), and with aid sent from nations all over the world.

In less than a year's time, the result was called "little less than a miracle." Nothing quite like it had ever taken place.

The principal leader of the rebellion, Colonel Odumegwu Ojukwu, fled to exile in the Ivory Coast at the end of the conflict. And a British diplomat remarked of General Gowon, "He won the peace by not acting as if he had won the war."

It seemed that Africa's most populous and one of its wealthiest countries might after all become the leader of the black African nations, as so many around the world had either been hoping—or fearing.

The Face of the Land

Nigeria's greatest geographical distinction is the fact that it supports by far the largest population of any country in Africa. These people live in an area of 356,669 square miles—covering about the same size as the states of Texas and Oklahoma combined. Nigeria is the largest coastal state of West Africa.

The 475 miles of coastline along the Gulf of Guinea is dwarfed by the 2,500-mile land frontier where Nigeria meets its four neighboring countries—Benin to the

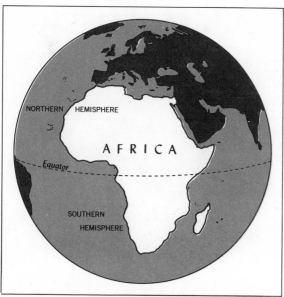

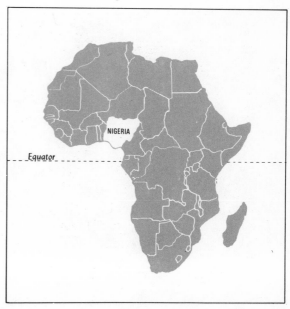

west, Niger and Chad on the north, and Cameroon on the east.

FROM TROPICS TO DESERT

Lying just behind the swaying palms of the coast are treacherous mangrove swamps, reaching as much as twenty miles inland in some places. The region is frequently cut by sluggish creeks and sand spits. Much of the area consists of freshwater lagoons, often interconnected. Surrounding the swamps and extending farther inland are the regions of tropical rain forest and oil-palm bush. This region is fifty to one hundred miles wide in many places.

The Niger River cuts through the country from the northwest to the coast, creating at its mouth the vast, muddy, half-land-half-water Niger delta. This ever-changing region is built of soil washed from much of West Africa by the great river and dumped near the river's mouth. There the river splits into many sluggish branches before it reaches the sea. This delta is one of the principal natural features of the entire west coast of Africa and covers an area of about 10,000 square miles.

Although much of the delta region is laced by the many fingers of the river, by lagoons, and by swamps, homes and some communities have been built in a few higher areas that are almost like islands.

Above the delta begins the lower Niger valley. Here, rich farmlands are cultivated intensively during the low-water period. At high water, the river can rise as much as thirty feet, covering much of the region and providing fertile new soil and moisture for the next crops, much as the Nile River has been doing in Egypt for thousands of years.

The lower Niger valley extends for about 185 miles north to the meeting place of the Niger and Benue rivers at Lokoja. From there, the combined valleys of the two rivers make up one of Nigeria's most unusually shaped geographic regions. The rather narrow Niger-Benue valley extends across the entire width of the country from east to west, dividing the north from the south.

The boundary with Cameroon is made up mostly of mountainous country known as the Eastern Highlands. Included here are ranges of 3,000- to 4,000-foot elevations such as the Obudu Uplands and the Shebshi Hills.

Vogel Peak, in the Shebshi Hills, is the highest-known spot in all of Nigeria. But its elevation is only about 6,800 feet; Nigeria has no really outstanding mountain peaks.

Other regions south of the Niger-Benue valley are the Western High Plains, the

A group of Nigerians prepare their boat for a twilight fishing trip on Lagos Lagoon, one of the countless lagoons that dot the Nigerian countryside. These lagoons are used for recreation as well as for fishing.

UNITED NATIONS

11

Southeastern Scarplands—where fascinating rock formations have been left by erosion—and the Southeastern Lowlands.

In the north the country grows increasingly dry and desert-like. The major part of the northern section is known as the Northern High Plains. Within these plains is the Jos Plateau. Its higher elevations, cooler weather, and different natural vegetation set it apart as a separate region.

East of the Northern High Plains is the low, gently sloping land of the Chad Basin, which extends all the way to Lake Chad on Nigeria's far northeastern border. West of the Northern High Plains are the Sokoto Plains. This flat area is broken up by deep riverbeds which are full—even to flooding—only in the rainy season.

Between the coast and the Sokoto Plains are the Western High Plains. This land formation extends across all of West Africa, and is a fertile agricultural region.

THE WATERS OF NIGERIA

One of Nigeria's principal geographic features—the one responsible for its name—is the great Niger River, third largest on the continent. Before it reaches the northwestern border of Nigeria, the Niger has already traveled 1,800 miles through five other countries of Africa. It meanders across Nigeria for another 730 miles.

The Niger River enters Nigeria on the Benin border and flows mostly to the east until it meets its greatest tributary, the Benue. There it makes an abrupt turn and flows almost directly south emptying into the Gulf of Guinea.

The Benue River enters Nigeria on the Cameroon border, and flows for almost 500 miles before becoming a part of the Niger.

Nigeria has a rather complex drainage pattern. In the southwest a divide separates

MAP KEY

Abakaliki, F3
Abuja, D3
Apapa, D4
Argungu, B1
Asaba, F3

Badagri, E1
Badagry Creek, E1
Benue River, D4
Bonny, F3
Borgu Game Reserve, D1

Calabar, F4
Chad Basin, B6
Chad Lake, B6
Cross River, F3

Eastern Highlands, E5
Enugu, E3

Gongola River, D5
Guinea, Gulf of, F1

Ibadan, E1
Ife, E1
Ikoyi, E1
Ilorin, E1

Jebba, D1
Jos, D4
Jos Plateau, D4

Kaduna, C3
Kaduna River, D2
Kainji Lake, D2
Kano, C4
Katsina Ala River, E4
Koko, C2
Komadugu-Yobe River, B5

Lagos, E1
Lokoja, E3

Maiduguri, C6

Niger River, C1
Nok, E3
Northern High Plains, C2
Nsukka, E3

Obudu Uplands, E4
Ogbomosho, E1
Oloibiri, F3
Onitsha, F3
Oshogbo, E2
Owerri, F3
Oyo, E1

Port Harcourt, F3

Shebshi Hills, D5
Sokoto Plains, C2
Sokoto River, C2
Southeastern Lowlands, F3
Southeastern Scarplands, F4

Vogel Peak, D5

Warri, F2
Western High Plains, D1

Yankari Game Reserve, D4
Yelwa, C2
Yola, D5

Zaria, C3
Zurak, D5

the waters. Tributaries to the north flow to the Niger. Smaller independent rivers to the south flow directly into the Gulf of Guinea or into the many lagoons along the coast. One of these, flowing from Cameroon to the eastern Nigerian coast, is the Cross. Its fame derives from the days of the slave trade and other "commerce."

Rains falling on the mysterious Jos Plateau flow both north and south. South-flowing waters from the Jos Plateau fill major tributaries of the Niger, including the Sokoto and Kaduna, and of the Benue, including the Gongola. To the north, the waters of the Jos Plateau form the Komadugu-Yobe River, fed by several tributaries. Its riverbed extends to Lake Chad, but since so much of the water in the Komadugu-Yobe evaporates or seeps into the ground, only a trickle reaches the lake. During the dry season, the northern part of the Komadugu-Yobe becomes merely a series of ponds.

NATURAL AND ARTIFICIAL

Lake Chad is one of the more unusual of the world's freshwater bodies. Most maps do not even attempt to locate its exact boundaries. During the dry season, Lake Chad may lose almost half of its total size. In December and January it shrinks from 10,000 square miles to a little more than 5,000.

In addition to Nigeria, Lake Chad borders on Niger and the country of Chad, which took its name from the lake. Most of the lake's shrinkage during the dry season takes place on the flat plains of the Nigerian side, and very little of the water in the lake comes from Nigeria.

Generators in the Kainji Dam began producing electricity for commercial use in 1968.

UNITED NATIONS

The other major body of water in Nigeria is Kainji Lake. This artificial lake resulted from the damming of the Niger River near Kainji, above Jebba. It fills the river valley for about 85 miles upstream, extending in width from 9 to 15 miles and covering an area of 480 square miles.

After the dam was completed, the lake filled to capacity in the short time from August to October 1968. The 45,000 people who lived in the 135 towns and villages now under water were resettled in new communities built either along the lake or inland.

CLIMATE

Because so many Europeans could not survive the heat, high humidity, and unique diseases of this tropical region, Nigeria gained a reputation as the "white man's graveyard." Today, of course, modern medicine has changed this.

All of Nigeria can be classified as tropical. However, south of the meeting place of the Niger and Benue rivers, Nigeria experiences four rather distinct seasons. There is a long dry season, followed by a long rainy season, a short period of less rain, and finally a short period of heavy rains. Average temperatures are about 71 to 73 degrees. They stay about the same all year, especially near the coast.

Along the coast as much as 140 inches of rain fall each year. Rainfall gradually diminishes toward the north. In the extreme northeast, total rainfall is less than twenty inches per year, except in the high Jos Plateau. There 60 to 80 inches of rain fall each year.

The entire north averages twenty to thirty inches of rain per year, but most of this falls during a short span of time. Parts of the north may endure as long as five to seven months without rain. During this long dry time wells dry up, streams run dry, and many areas are almost entirely without water. When the rainy season finally comes, much of the rain that does fall runs off without benefiting the land. Temperatures are high too, especially in March and April. Average high temperatures can be 101 to 105 degrees in those months and from 91 to 94 degrees for the year.

Four Children of Nigeria

FLORA OF JOS

Standing far away, and some distance behind her father, Flora watched as figures in the circle stepped to the rhythm of the drums. Flora was watching a traditional funeral dance of the Kaleri people, and she was excited! These old dances are fast dying out and there are fewer and fewer opportunities to see them performed at a Kaleri gathering.

Flora is very much part of the new ways of life in Nigeria. She and her father and mother live in a pleasant, modern house on the outskirts of the city of Jos. Friends from the United States who sometimes visit them are surprised that the house has a fireplace, which the family often uses in the cool evenings. Jos is situated on a high plateau, and its pleasant climate is much different from the hot, dry north or the tropical south.

Flora enjoys watching performances by colorfully costumed dancers like these.

MINISTRY OF INFORMATION

17

Flora's father is descended from the Tiv people, most of whom live somewhat to the south, and her mother comes from an ancient people known as the Mama group. They have lived in the plateau area since prehistoric times and are known in Nigeria as the "Old People." Until recently the Jos Plateau was very isolated, so the Old People have kept their traditional ways longer than most of Nigeria's other peoples.

Although it lies in such an old region, Jos itself is a rather young city. It sprang up rather quickly as a mining boom town when tin was discovered in the region. Flora's grandfather came to Jos from his nearby native village of Miango to work in the tin mines nearby. He was one of the first to leave the village for a "modern" job. Some of the Americans who helped supervise the newly opened mines said that Jos was very much like early mining towns in the western United States. When he told Flora this, she was very interested because she has heard a lot about the United States from her parents' American friends. Her grandfather, though, was not quite sure what the Americans were talking about.

Now Flora's grandfather has retired from the mines. He has a small farm near Jos, where he grows mostly sorghum, a cereal plant similar to corn.

Flora's mother was one of the best students in her school in Jos. When she graduated, she was selected to study nursing at the University of Ibadan far away in southern Nigeria. While she was growing up, she knew of many people who had died because there were just not enough medicines and trained people to help them. She wanted to do whatever she could to help these people. The opportunity to study nursing at the university was also a great honor as well.

At the university, she met Flora's father. He was studying mining engineering. They married and returned to Jos where Flora's father had a supervisory job in the mines.

While Flora was still a little girl, her father began to study the traditions and legends of the Old People as a hobby. Soon he became quite an authority. Finally, he applied for a scholarship offered by an international education agency to study in the United States. He left his family at Jos and received his degree in anthropology from an American university. Now he works as an assistant in the fine small museum at Jos.

Flora attends a good modern school, but gets a different kind of education when her father lets her join him on his field trips. She loves to travel to the tiny, remote villages where the houses are made of *pisa,* an unbaked clay, and topped by straw-thatched roofs.

On one of these trips Flora's father took her to the little village of Nok, near where the Niger and Benue rivers meet. It was here that some of the most exciting discoveries of African archaeology were found. The Nok were the first people to live in the Jos region. Near the village were discovered ceramic sculptures made by these prehistoric people. Many of the finest of these are exhibited at the museum in Jos, and

Buildings at the Bilingual Center for the Training of Museum Technicians in Jos are built in traditional shapes. Perhaps Flora will attend this school if her interest in the history of Nigeria continues.

Flora loves to visit the museum and carefully study each of the exhibits.

Flora is afraid that by the time she grows up the old traditions will have disappeared from the villages of the plateau. Even now, more and more of the people are going to the cities, and modern ways are replacing the old in the villages.

That is why her father is working so long and hard to learn as much as he can from the older members of the region's peoples. This work is very difficult and often requires Flora's father to be away from his family. Because none of the groups had written languages, all the traditional tales and customs were passed from one generation to another by word of mouth. Now Flora's father must hear them so he can write them down or tape-record them.

Although her father can speak several local languages and dialects, Flora will have to wait until she is older to take such courses in school. There are so many groups and languages in the Jos region that

19

only English, Nigeria's official language, is taught in the lower grades. However, on field trips she has picked up some local words and phrases. Local people such as the Kaleri are delighted when she can greet them with a cheerful word or phrase in their own language. *"Zaki"* is a Kaleri greeting, and Flora enjoys saying it and hearing it every time she meets a Kaleri person.

Flora can hardly wait until she can become an anthropologist, too. Or perhaps she'll be an archaeologist, so she can study the ancient peoples of Nigeria. University is a long time off, though, so Flora just keeps on doing her homework.

YAKUBU OF LAGOS

Yakubu will never forget the day he met the former head of the federal military government. The great man shook hands kindly and then smiled very broadly when Yakubu's father mentioned his son's name. He gave a friendly nod to the father and patted the boy on the back. Yakubu was very proud that his parents had named him in honor of their country's long-time leader and commander-in-chief of the armed forces.

Yakubu is a Yoruba, and his name is not a traditional one of the group, the second largest in Nigeria. However, his parents admired their country's leader so much that they named their eldest son in honor of General Yakubu Gowon. Many children of Yakubu's age share this name.

Through his father, Yakubu is descended from a long line of Yoruba noblemen. They dealt with British traders in the early days and accumulated a family fortune through trading and later in their large stores in several Yoruba towns of southwestern Nigeria. Yakubu's father studied governmental administration at one of England's finest universities. He currently serves on Nigeria's National Universities Commission. After a few more years of experience, he will probably move into positions of greater importance in the government.

Yakubu loves his native city of Lagos and already he knows almost every part of it thoroughly. Being a rather venturesome boy, he often braves his father's anger by doing some exploring on his own, such as the time he took the ferry to the port of Apapa, or when he took a launch to Tarkwa Beach. Once Yakubu even saved his money and went on a special boat ride to explore the reaches of nearby Badagry Creek. Secretly, he thinks his father is somewhat proud of such exploits, even though his father "chews him out" (as Yakubu has heard Americans say) whenever he gets caught.

In spite of its great size, Yakubu knows and enjoys almost every inch of the Nigeria Museum. And he particularly loves to

Two views of Lagos. Top: This aerial view shows the mixture of old buildings with new skyscrapers. Bottom: Some of the streets in Lagos are just wide enough for a single car to get through.

roam Lagos's immense public market, watching the buyers and the merchants. Sometimes he brings home a particularly interesting potion or herb known as *juju* and he pretends to be a magician from a remote village. Many of Yakubu's countrymen still believe very strongly that the juju have special magical powers.

Yakubu's father's work has taken the family to all of the universities in Nigeria, but Yakubu especially enjoyed the time they went to the University of Ife. While there, the family paid a visit to the spiritual leader of the Yoruba people, the *oni* of Ife. When Yakubu went to the University of Ibadan with his father he had an opportunity to meet the great Nigerian playwright Wole Sokinka. Yakubu's father said that he thinks Sokinka is truly a genius.

Ikoyi, the island suburb of Lagos where Yakubu lives, has many fine homes owned mostly by wealthy Nigerians and important government officials. However, some members of Yakubu's family still live in the handsome old family compound in the city of Lagos itself, which is on another island, Iddo. The compound contains a number of houses grouped together within a walled enclosure. Everyone who lives in the compound is closely related to everyone else. This has been the customary way the Yoruba people have lived.

Yakubu's mother is very involved with various groups that do social and welfare work. Yakubu has gone with her on a number of her frequent visits to the Yoruba villages that are just outside Lagos, where many of the older people need special care and attention.

Yakubu's favorite activities are music and sports, and he'd have a hard time choosing which he likes better. Though many of his friends listen only to European and American popular music, Yakubu likes Nigerian folk music as well. He is a member of a young people's choral group which, along with an adult chorus, presents several programs a year of the traditional songs and chants. Sometimes they join with dance groups and small ensembles where traditional instruments are played. Yakubu also listens to Nigerian folk music on the national radio network.

Soccer is Yakubu's favorite sport, and he never misses an opportunity to play or to watch some of the organized teams play. He has seen professional baseball games in the United States and attended a rugby match when the family visited England, but soccer is his favorite. Nigeria does not permit professional sports, and Yakubu has a hard time understanding this. His father, who is on the local Sports Council, says that Nigeria prefers to encourage competition and health in sports.

Yakubu and his father sometimes work together on some of the traditional crafts in a special small room they've put together. Sometimes the two of them go to the city of Oyo, north of Lagos. Here Yakubu can watch some of the most skillful leather workers, weavers, wood sculptors, and calabash (gourd) carvers of the Yoruba people at work. Yakubu is taking lessons in calabash carving.

Yakubu saw exciting pieces of artwork like this one at the International Black Arts Festival.

Yakubu had a chance to see a tremendous variety of crafts from all over Africa and much of the rest of the world when the family attended the International Festival of Black Arts and Culture at Lagos in 1977. Yakubu was very proud that his country was the host of this fine festival, and was especially happy when his father took him to the festival for a second visit.

He and all of his family love to attend as many of Nigeria's colorful annual festivals as possible. During the family's visit to Ife they attended the annual festival that celebrates the ancient religion of the Yoruba people. Yakubu was fascinated by the elaborate traditional dances. He knew some of the music from singing with his choral group.

Yakubu's family have often cheered the spectacle of the Egungun festivals at Ibadan and Oshogbo. Once they even made a special trip north to Kano to see the Muslim festivals held at the end of the month of Ramadan.

When they visited Oshogbo, Yakubu was a little afraid of the strange forest shrines with their weird sculptures and monuments, but he remembered his calabash carvings and made sketches of some of the designs to use on his calabashes. He was also somewhat afraid when they visited the famous European priestess of Oshun, but her house and the extraordinary pieces of sculpture she was working on made him forget his fears.

Yakubu and his parents especially enjoy

going to the Cathay Restaurant in Lagos and trying the exotic Chinese dishes. Yakubu's father says they are the best examples of Chinese food to be found in all Africa. However, Yakubu would prefer to eat the dishes he knows best—the simple traditional dishes such as foofoo, garri, cocoyam, plantain, and guinea corn. Of course, their excellent cook also prepares foods from almost every nation for the family's many guests.

Yakubu has not decided what he wants to do, and his mind is in quite a whirl. Right now he is deciding whether to be a doctor, a government officer like his father, an artist, a musician, or an executive in the family business. One thing he is sure of: he will attend one of Nigeria's fine universities and then go to the United States or England for further study. Maybe by then, he muses, he'll have made a decision about his career.

ELIZABETH OF OWERRI

Elizabeth was only a tiny baby so she does not remember the terrible war. Her mother does not talk about it much anymore because it makes her very sad. But Elizabeth knows how much different her life might have been if there had been no war.

Both her father and mother were descended from the Ibo line. Almost as soon as the terrible civil war began, Elizabeth's father went off to fight so that the Ibo region called Biafra would become an independent nation. Her mother never saw him again.

Before long, the war engulfed their own city of Owerri. Elizabeth's mother had to flee the city with her baby. She took refuge with some members of her family in a safe place far from the fighting.

Elizabeth remembers when she and her mother came back to Owerri. She remembers how her mother gasped and cried when she saw how much of her hometown had been destroyed by war. Young as she was, Elizabeth too remembers the gaping holes in the ground, the empty foundations, the charred timbers, and the complete desolation.

There was nothing left of their home at all, so they lived in a temporary barracks-like tent. General Yakubu Gowon's troops were everywhere, and at first the people were afraid that they would be treated badly because they had started and lost a terrible war.

But the troops carefully followed General Gowon's strict orders. They prevented disorder and helped to distribute the emergency food and medical supplies that were pouring in from the Nigerian government and from relief agencies all over the world. They also enforced strict sanitary measures and operated the emergency health services which kept epidemics and disease under control.

Though Elizabeth's family had made a habit of regularly saving the profits from their small store, they were afraid that the good-sized savings account they had accumulated was gone now. But to their joy, they learned that the government had preserved these accounts and was now returning them to their rightful owners.

Before Elizabeth was born, her mother and father had lived for a while in the northern city of Maiduguri. There they set up a small store in the section known in the Hausa language as the *sabon gari* or "new town." This is what the Muslim people of the north call the newer portions of a city where the non-Muslims live.

The Hausa and Fulani peoples of the north had become alarmed at the great numbers of newcomers. They felt that the newcomers, especially the Ibo newcomers, were taking over too much of the business and trying to gain control. So there were riots and attacks on the people of the sabon gari sections in many of the cities of the north; the Ibo people were special targets of these attacks. After several of their Ibo friends and acquaintances had been killed, Elizabeth's mother and father fled back to Owerri. They borrowed money from the local Improvement Union to set up a small store, which rapidly prospered.

Money from the government added to some of her savings helped Elizabeth's mother to re-establish the store. Because the Improvement Union had helped her so much, she became active in helping to revive the Union. It is a cooperative group that helps all its members, but gives special assistance to the most needy.

Relief materials for Elizabeth's people were supplied by the Nigerian government and by countries around the world.

MINISTRY OF INFORMATION

No one who knows Elizabeth's mother is surprised at her success. Ibo women traditionally have been the most independent and most respected of all the women of western Africa. If Elizabeth's mother had lived a few generations earlier, and Elizabeth's father had still been living, as her wealth increased she might have "bought" additional brides for her husband. These would have served as babysitters and secretaries for the husband and the first wife. A woman who had the wealth required to do this had great prestige. Elizabeth is very proud of her mother's success, and one of her favorite after-school activities is reading about some of the early Nigerian women who were especially successful in trade and business.

Elizabeth's mother uses much of her money to save for her daughter's education and to give liberally to charitable causes through the Episcopalian church. Ancestors on both sides of Elizabeth's family were among the first of the Nigerian people to become Christians.

A favorite phrase among the Ibo is "getting up"; it means making a success of oneself. Many Ibo have done just this, achieving high places in business and government. Elizabeth wants to be one of them, so she works hard in the fine new school which is part of restored Owerri. She studies arithmetic, writing, reading, dictation, nature study, scripture, history, geography, drawing, handwork, health science, English, and the Ibo language. After primary school she will attend secondary school for five years to obtain the School Certificate, and then another two years for the Higher School Certificate. Her college education will take three more years.

A number of Nigerian women have held high posts in the government, such as Cabinet Member (Commissioner), High Court Judge, and Permanent Secretary in one or another ministry. Elizabeth admires these women very much. She plans to study law and either practice law privately or try for a career in public service. Elizabeth knows the government needs honest and dedicated officials and she hopes that maybe someday she can be one of them.

MOHAMMED OF KANO

Mohammed's father is descended from a long line of the Fulani nobility. The Fulani group, with its many subgroups, is the largest ethnic group in Nigeria. In feature and build, Mohammed and his father are both slim, with light bronze skin and fine features. The Fulani believe they come from North Africa, and many of them—like many North Africans—have a somewhat Arab appearance.

Mohammed's mother is descended from an even more lengthy line of Hausa merchants. Many Hausa also live in neighboring Chad and Niger. For many generations, the Hausa-Fulani peoples have ruled and provided the primary language in the northern section of what is now Nigeria.

The city of Kano is the largest in what

people who practice the Muslim religion call the "holy north" of Nigeria. Here is the largest *mosque,* Muslim place of worship, in all Nigeria. Mohammed's father is an official at the court of the Emir of Kano. The Emir is an important spiritual leader as well as a traditional political leader. He carries on his semi-official functions from his great and beautiful palace in the old section of Kano. Mohammed's family is quite important in the town. They and their many servants live in one of the other large residences of the old city. Of course their home is not quite as large and imposing as the palace itself.

Mohammed's father is a devoted scholar of the *Koran,* the Muslim holy book. He has studied Arabic for many years and he is one of the very few Nigerians who comes close to understanding the original text of the Koran. Mohammed hopes that someday he can be as knowledgeable about his religion as his father. To that end, he studies hard at the Koranic school that he attends in the late afternoons. There he learns the Arabic language and starts on what can become a lifelong study of his religion's holy book. During most of the day Mohammed attends Wazirci Ward Primary School, where he learns languages, science, mathematics, and many other subjects. He enjoys school very much.

Mohammed thinks the modern mosque at Kano, built of snow-white stone, with a blue-green dome and gleaming white minarets, is one of the finest buildings he has ever seen. Sometimes Mohammed joins Muslims and nonbelievers alike to climb

This girl, like Mohammed, is a Fulani.

the 103 spiraled steps to the top of one of the minarets. From there, he can look out over the sea of mud houses that is Kano. Sometimes he even spots a camel caravan on the far-off desert, or else a donkey train bringing in a load of peanuts or carrying out dyed goatskins to be sold in northern Africa as "Morocco" leather. More often, though, he sees a more modern sight— trucks on the desert roads and airplanes overhead. Both are replacing the old, slow methods of transport.

Prayer is one of the five fundamental pious duties of the Muslim faith which are called the Five Pillars of Islam. Mohammed and his family pray faithfully five times a day, facing toward the holy city of Mecca. The midday-Friday prayers are most important of all, and Mohammed loves to mingle with the faithful who gath-

27

Mohammed worships in a stately white mosque like this one.

er at the mosque for these special prayers. Sometimes the throngs swell to as many as 10,000 people.

A pilgrimage to Mecca, the holy city of the Muslims located in Saudi Arabia, is the goal of every Muslim believer. Mohammed hopes to make this pilgrimage some day.

Another of Mohammed's favorite places is Kano's colorful market. He likes to see the market women gracefully carrying burdens on their heads; some may balance as many as four huge calabashes each as big as two feet in diameter. Some girls carry their whole stock of goods on their heads, in a sort of mobile department store, and move about from place to place in the market. Others have more formal booths,

displaying the textiles, leather goods, carved calabashes, wood carvings, every variety of food, and other delights of the huge market. One of the most popular items is kola nuts from the south. These are chewed as a kind of stimulant. Another "treat" is *halawa*, a kind of sugar candy pulled like taffy.

Mingling with the crowd may be some of the colorful men from the desert. Many of these may be among the horsemen who gather for the great festival at Kano after the Muslim month of Ramadan.

At the festival there will be acrobats and snake dancers and magicians and music and dancing and wonderful barbecues of sheep meat. But most of all Mohammed will love to watch the brilliant horsemanship of the desert leaders. His father rides with them, and Mohammed thinks his father is just about the most dashing of the riders, many of whom have just about the most fantastic costumes Mohammed can imagine.

The riders' heads are enveloped in turbans of yard after yard of fluffy materials in the brightest of reds, yellows, greens, and other colors. Their bodies are swathed in many layers of equally brilliant colored robes, covered with quilted overlaid and embroidered designs in fantastic array. Their horses have at least four or five decorated and fringed saddle blankets and many other fancy trappings. Of course, these costumes are only worn for festive occasions.

One of the most exciting features of the festival is the traditional charge of the horsemen as they dash forward waving their spears. Some of them wear chain mail, with their horses protected by "armor" of quilted cloth. This was one of the most effective maneuvers of warfare in North Africa of an earlier day.

Mohammed's father also uses his excellent horsemanship to play the more modern game of polo. Mohammed can hardly wait until he is old enough to play on a team. He already is almost as good a horseman as his father, and the older man thinks someday he will be even better. Father and son make a very dashing team as they streak across the countryside on their beautiful mounts.

Mohammed's family also owns several expensive modern European cars, which they frequently use to take overland trips. One of the most interesting of these was

Wooden carvings like the ones this craftsman is creating are sold in Kano's marketplace.

the drive from Kano to N'Djamena (formerly called Fort Lamy), the capital of neighboring Chad. On the way, they visited with a number of the Muslim desert leaders who were all well known to the family.

The family has done a great deal more traveling together. At least twice a year they go to Europe or the United States, perhaps alternating to South America. They have also visited Iran and Saudi Arabia. But while he likes the larger foreign cities, Mohammed still thinks his own Kano is the most interesting. One of his hobbies is reading about the long history of his great desert metropolis, and he can recite all the reasons why it has remained important for over a thousand years.

Unlike many of the women of the north, Mohammed's mother does not veil her face and play an inconspicuous role. She is one of the leaders in the growing group of Muslim women who want a more independent and individual way of life, and her husband agrees with her completely. Both the law and their religion would permit him to have other wives, but he does not intend to do so.

Many other customs are changing also among the Fulani. For many years the cruel custom of *sharo* has been forbidden by law. This is a ceremony that is said to be the "initiation" rite of Fulani boys, the time when they are accepted as men of their group or when they are ready for marriage.

Mohammed has heard that the sharo still takes place occasionally, despite being outlawed, and he would like to see it. Secretly, he feels sure he could stand up to this severe test even though he is not accustomed to the rugged nomadic life. In the sharo, the boy-man stands rigid, with face muscles taut; all around are his friends, the young girls, and other neighbors and acquaintances, watching him intently. He may be holding a mirror high above his head to see that he does not flinch or change his facial expression in any way.

Another boy his age, often his best friend, takes a heavy stick and beats the initiate's back forcefully, sometimes bringing considerable blood. The candidate must not show any sign of fear or emotion. Sometimes coins are pressed against his forehead. If they stick to his skin, this will be an indication of perspiration, and he will fail the test. Most of the boys pass on the first test; a few must take the test again. If they fail a second time they are disgraced, especially in the eyes of the girls.

Although he will never have to prove his manhood in this way, Mohammed knows that there will be many other opportunities for him to use the traditional courage and ability of his people, no matter what kind of life he makes for himself.

In some ways Flora, Yakubu, Elizabeth, and Mohammed might seem like exceptional young people, but they represent the kinds of privileges and opportunities available to so many of Nigeria's young people, more now than ever before.

30

Nigeria Yesterday

THE NOK

The earliest civilization known in present-day Nigeria was developed to a rather high degree by a group known as the Nok peoples. Some experts say they were present as far back as 2000 B.C., although others say the Nok were at their height from about 500 B.C. to 200 A.D. The Nok lived north of where the Niger and Benue rivers meet, in an area about three hundred miles long and one hundred miles wide.

Nok culture was at about an Iron Age level. In addition to ironwork, the Nok also produced beautiful ceramic sculpture. The Nok usually are considered to be the ancestors of many of the peoples who still live in that part of Nigeria.

When the Nok civilization declined, there was no high degree of culture in the region until about the ninth century, when a new power, the Kanem-Borno empire, began to emerge in Chad and extend itself west into Nigeria. No one knows just where the majority of these northern people came from. Certainly some came from nearby Sudan; others undoubtedly made their way south from northern Africa, possibly even Egypt, and possibly from as far away as Yemen.

KANEM-BORNO

Whatever its origins, this Kanem-Borno empire became one of the great empires that flourished in the desert beginning in about the ninth century. Most of these empires were to the north and west of present-day Nigeria and looked to Timbuktu (now in Mali) as a center of culture.

By the early eleventh century Kanem's

A Hausa woman and her child, descendants of one of Nigeria's oldest peoples, sit in front of their grass hut.

rulers had come under the Muslim influence and by the end of that century the Kanem peoples had a Muslim king. Sometime in the twelfth century, the center of power in the area began to shift west from Kanem (in Chad) to Borno (in Nigeria). Eventually the Borno empire extended as far to the west as the Hausa states of Kano and Katsina.

Borno power declined during the fourteenth century, but it revived strongly in the sixteenth century during the reign of Mai Idris. He renewed the power of Borno in the east as far as what is now the Darfur region of western Sudan.

Then the Borno empire began another decline which lasted almost three hundred years. In the early nineteenth century, Borno surprisingly revived again, under the strength of a military leader who came from outside the area. His name was Mohammed al-Kanemi.

The rural people, mostly Fulani, were upset over what they saw as a breakdown of religious practice by the more urbanized people around them. Led by Utuman (or Usuman) Dan Fodio, a Muslim soldier, they started a *jihad* (holy war) against both the Borno empire and the Hausa city-states. Borno, under the leadership of Mohammed Al-Kanemi, resisted the invaders. However, the city-states of the Hausa were conquered, and the Sokoto Caliphate was begun.

HAUSA-FULANI

The early history of the Hausa states of the north is not too well known, though today the Hausa-Fulani are the largest ethnic group in Nigeria. They probably began in about the tenth century, but in all their history they never moved together to become an empire, unlike so many of their neighbors. As a result they experienced many difficulties in their relations with these neighbors.

Sometimes the Hausa were overrun by invaders from the west; at other periods they paid tribute to Borno and once were conquered by the Songhai empire. Their powers were mostly of the "city-state" type, also found in Europe during the medieval period. Even today, Kano still has remains of ancient walls of thick earthen construction. For centuries Kano's ornamented streets and twisting lanes teemed with the commerce that made it a center of trade and politics which sometimes even rivaled Timbuktu.

The Hausa were successfully conquered by Utuman Dan Fodio and his Fulani cavalry between 1804 and 1810. However, the Hausa language continued to be the *lingua franca* (common language) of trade in West Africa. The conquering people formed the Sokoto Caliphate in their new territory and extended their realm and their religion far to the south and west.

Walls surrounding the "old city" of Kano were originally built to serve as protection against the cities' enemies.

THE YORUBA

The region that is now southwestern Nigeria was long dominated by the Yoruba peoples.

Their legends say that they originated at Ife, which remains their religious center even today.

Because they had no written language, little is known about the early Yoruba peoples. However, their statues of cast bronze found at Ife and some other locations are ranked among the best such work produced anywhere. The fine terra-cotta portrait heads of Ife also indicate that the early civilization of the Yoruba had advanced to a high degree. Much of this art dates from the twelfth through the fourteenth centuries, and some examples of it can be seen in Nigerian museums.

Two main kingdoms arose from the Yoruba peoples—the Oyo and the Benin. During the 1400s both Oyo and Benin power expanded. The Benin kingdom reached its peak in the early sixteenth century. It obtained great power because it was the only group in the area with firearms. It got them by trading with the Portuguese.

As Benin power declined, the Oyo kingdoms became more important and much larger until it reached its peak probably about the mid-1700s. Its borders touched the present-day Benin nation on the west,

Religious and decorative artifacts of the Yoruba people tell many things about Yoruba history and religion, including the various gods and spirits in which they believed.

the Hausa city-states on the north, and even some of the coastal ports.

But by the mid-1800s, both empires had declined. The Ibo and Ijaw dynasties took over the Benin's hold on Niger delta trade. The separate states of Ibadan, Kjaiye, Ijebu, and Abeokuta became the successors to the once-mighty Oyo empire. To the east the most powerful trading group were the Efik, in their center at Old Calabar. However, they never had a strong government and before long the coastal areas were dominated by trade with the Europeans.

EUROPEAN BEGINNINGS

The first European explorers in West Africa were the Portuguese. When they first arrived, in the late fifteenth century, they only wanted to get around the coast of Africa to the riches of the Far East. Soon, however, the Portuguese began to see how important West Africa's slaves, gold, and ivory would be. They built a fortress at Elmina on the Gold Coast (now Ghana) to protect their trade monopoly in that area, and they remained in control for over a century. In 1486, they established their first stronghold in what is now Nigeria, near present-day Benin.

In the early seventeenth century the Dutch took over most of the Portuguese settlements and power in West Africa. But by the mid-1700s, however, France and England began to control trade in much of the coastal area. The traders themselves did not go very far inland, but trade from the interior with the coast increased substantially over the years.

SLAVERY AND SALVATION

Most of the early trading was in human misery. Slavery had been carried on for generations in the area, long before the Europeans ever arrived. Some slaves had been kept for work in the region, but most were sold to Arab traders.

However, as European settlements in the New World grew, the demand for slaves to work the Western Hemisphere plantations increased enormously. Most of the local rulers of West Africa were quite willing to meet this demand. As one author has pointed out, "Africans were no less guilty in the slave trade" than the Europeans.

In fact, many local chieftains and traders had grown wealthy on their monopoly of the trade in slaves with the Europeans. From its beginnings in the early 1500s to its tapering off as late as 1860, it is estimated that more than six million human beings were shipped into slavery from West Africa alone.

Gradually, of course, the Western nations turned away from slavery. European and Western Hemisphere governments began to pass and enforce laws against the owning of one person by another. Slave traders found they could no longer become as wealthy from the trade. By the late nineteenth century the slave trade to the West had almost ceased.

One reason the slave trade became so

important was that the area that is now Nigeria produced little else that could be sold to the outside world. However, palm oil, cocoa beans, and other local products showed promise, and by the early 1800s the Niger River port of Bonny had become the leading palm-oil market of Africa. Trade was often precarious and difficult, though, since neither the traders nor the local chiefs had any central authority to which they could bring serious problems or disputes. So the British appointed John Beecroft as consul to the coastal region of present-day Nigeria. He was well respected by Africans and Europeans alike. To develop further the export of African products, in 1879 Britain's Sir George Goldie founded the United Africa Company, which became the Royal Niger Company in 1886.

For many years the company monopolized trade and was a semi-official ruling force in the area for Britain.

his entire company died on this expedition because of disease and other troubles, but his notebooks contained important information about the West African interior that was to be used by explorers who came later.

Other explorers, such as Macgregor Laird and Heinrich Barth (who went through northern Nigeria) opened the way for trade with the people of Nigeria's interior. The Royal Niger Company used the routes opened up by these explorers to build on their own trade monopoly within the area.

Not only the Europeans became wealthy during this period. Many fortunes were built among the local people. One of these, a woman known as Madame Tinubu, became famous because she had more power than many of the local kings and chiefs. Many African women became wealthy and influential traders, but all the European traders were men.

EXPLORING THE NIGER

Traders brought stories back to Europe of the mysterious Niger River, whose course and source were unknown. A famous Scottish explorer named Mungo Park came to the upper Niger in 1796 and four years later led another expedition up the Niger. However, until quinine began to be used in the mid-eighteenth century, trade with the people of the upper Niger and Benue rivers was limited because so many traders died of malaria. Mungo Park and

THE NEW RELIGION

Throughout Africa, Christian missionaries usually arrived not long after trade was established with Europeans. Stories would come back to Europe about how the Africans lived and worshiped. The missionaries, who usually had something of the explorer's instinct, would see newly opened parts of Africa as fertile new ground for their work. So it was in Nigeria. Yet as late as in the 1840s, Christian missionary work was confined almost entirely to the western coastal areas where the Yoruba lived. The work there expanded rapidly until by 1880 there were 6,000 Christian believers among the Yoruba and as many as 17,000 by 1910. Later, missionaries moved east to the Ibo, who were particularly receptive to this new religion. In 1910 there were 18,500 Ibo Christians. In 1920 there were 500,000! Many of these were Roman Catholic. Missionaries attempted to move north into the interior but were frustrated there because the Islamic religion was so strong.

The missionaries realized that in order for Christianity to become an important force in Africa there would have to be native African religious leaders. By 1894, in one important missionary group, two-thirds of the clergy were African. A one-time Yoruba slave, Samuel Adjai Crowther, was freed, received his early education in Sierra Leone, then became the first Nigerian to be schooled in England. He returned to Nigeria as a missionary and became one of Nigeria's best-known and revered religious leaders.

Samuel Crowther became the first bishop from among the local peoples. He was received by Queen Victoria, translated the New Testament into the Yoruba language, and worked and lived until almost ninety years of age.

BRITISH RULE

As trade and missionary activity increased, so did British influence. But the

NEW FRONTIERS IN THE CENTRAL SUDAN

An early Christian missionary holds an outdoor religious service.

government attempted to work as much as possible through the local leaders. The British had already used their navy and the Royal Niger Company to work against the slave trade and to protect British missionaries. However, very few British subjects wanted to settle in Nigeria. Britain felt it would be unnecessary to formally colonize Nigeria when trade was already so well established. All that changed toward the end of the nineteenth century when conflict arose among the European nations over their areas of influence in Africa. The Conference of Berlin, in 1885, set the stage for Britain's protectorate of present-day Nigeria's coastal area. Lagos had already been taken over as early as 1861 and

Local leaders called emirs, *like these men, were given control of local governments by the British colonial rulers in 1900. This was one of the first moves toward Nigerian independence.*

by 1874 was part of Britain's Gold Coast colony. In 1885, Britain established the Oil Rivers Protectorate which extended from Old Calabar (at the present-day Cameroon border) to the Niger delta. In 1893 the protectorate was extended to Lagos and up the Niger to Lokoja. Its name was changed to the Niger Coast Protectorate. Local kings, who had signed treaties with the British, still did most of the day-to-day governing.

In 1900 northern Nigeria officially became a protectorate of the British crown, which took over from the Royal Niger Company. However, day-to-day govern-

ment of the north was mostly under the control of its local leaders, known as *emirs.* They, in turn, reported to the British High Commissioner Frederick Lugard. This principle of *indirect rule* was used by Europeans to control many of their African holdings.

In 1906, southern Nigeria officially became a colony of Britain. Since most of the trade was in the south, it was much wealthier than the north and had much more contact with Europeans. So its industries and roads developed much faster.

In 1914, the British united the north and south into one colony. Now the north began to reap some of the south's wealth and the British brought their indirect rule to the south. When World War I began that year, Nigerians from both north and south served in the Royal West African Frontier Force.

After the war, Nigeria—like the rest of the world—prospered. The British established a constitution for their colony in 1922.

LEANINGS TOWARD NATIONHOOD

During the years between the two world wars a number of Nigerians began to work for more self-rule. Some who were the second and third generations of their families to attend school in Europe wanted to have more power in the many new cities that had sprung up. Others, especially many Ibo and Yoruba, wanted to make their own ethnic group the most important one. It was difficult for most British authorities to believe that the many different peoples in Nigeria could ever be united into one nation. One of the early leaders who did feel it could be done was Herbert Macauley, sometimes called "the father of Nigerian nationalism." He owned the *Lagos Daily News,* in which he wrote frequently in support of his views. In addition, he led Nigeria's most important political party.

The movement for independence was slow to reach Nigerians in small villages far away from the cities and towns.

The Nigerian National Democratic Party, Macauley's party, was concentrated almost entirely in the city of Lagos. Few people away from the city knew enough about politics to be interested. However, in the 1930s political activity increased and people outside Lagos began to take an interest in Nigerian nationalism.

Macauley dominated Nigerian politics until 1938, when the Nigerian Youth Movement (NYM) began to be the leading voice in Nigerian nationalism. This lasted only three years, though, as differences between Ibo and Yoruba NYM leaders interfered. Rivalry between these two ethnic groups persisted through the 1940s.

World War II brought large numbers of Americans to remote portions of Nigeria. Two divisions of Nigerians participated in the Asian and Middle East theaters of war. Such wartime experiences gave many Nigerians their first real international contacts and encouraged the movement toward independence. The current constitution, which had been enacted in 1922, provided very little power, elective or otherwise, for the natives of Nigeria. They wanted to feel that they had a greater voice in the administration of their government, and the British agreed with them. So the 1946 Richards Constitution created a national council that encompassed all of Nigeria and had a native Nigerian majority.

The Richards Constitution of 1946 was followed in five years by the Macpherson Constitution of 1951. It was named for the man who was then the governor of Nigeria. The next constitution, in 1954, sought to weld the north and south together firmly and pave the way for true independence. The British governor reduced the use of his powers and the national legislature received more authority.

Queen Elizabeth II made a triumphal 2,000-mile tour of her largest colony in 1956, in the midst of this movement toward independence. The visit provided one of the most colorful ceremonies of the century. The Muslim emirs and chieftains saluted the queen in the first *durbar* (gathering of local leaders in a British colony) to be held since one held in India in 1911. The splendidly robed and turbaned chiefs of the north and the magnificently and traditionally gowned leaders of the south and east tried to outdo one another in saluting the first British monarch ever to visit Nigeria—even though all knew that British authority soon would be coming to an end.

Nigeria Today

INDEPENDENCE

The eastern and western regions became self-governing in 1957, followed by the north in 1959. All three were still loosely attached to a central government at Lagos. The federation held powers that affected all of Nigeria, such as currency, defense, and foreign relations. All internal situations, though, were handled by the separate regions.

Constitutional conferences in London in 1957 and 1958 settled differences and made compromises between the various ethnic groups and regions. Discussions of many problems were long and difficult, but finally a constitution was agreed on.

On October 1, 1960, Nigeria became the sixteenth African colonial state to achieve independence, with a prime minister (Sir Abubakar Tafawa Balewa) and a governor general (Nnamdi Azikiwe) as the principal leaders of what was a rather loose federation.

Within two years, growing problems created the first major crisis of the new nation. Problems in the political party called the Action Group led to a state of emergency being declared in the Western Region from May 29 through December 31, 1962. The plan to create a fourth region, called the Mid-Western Region, further increased the political agitation.

On October 1, 1963, Nigeria changed its relationship to the British Commonwealth and proclaimed itself a Federal Republic, still retaining its Commonwealth ties. A new constitution was written and the establishment of the Mid-Western Region became a reality. The long-time nationalist leader Nnamdi Azikiwe was named the first president of the republic.

Instead of quieting the fears of various groups, the new changes resulted in even more rivalries and confusion. Each of Nigeria's four regions (north, west, east, and midwest) was dominated by a particular ethnic group that was represented by the region's major political party. In addition, each region had at least one ethnic minority group that was a majority in a neighboring region. The country was also viewed as being divided into north and south.

CIVIL STRIFE

In 1965 heavy rioting broke out in the Western Region. As many as 2,000 people were killed there between August 1965 and January 1966. Rioting and other disorders occurred elsewhere in the country, and on January 15, 1966, a small group of mostly Ibo army officers overthrew the government and assassinated Prime Minister Balewa and the premiers of the Northern and Western regions. General J.T.U. Aguiyi-Ironsi then formed a military government.

Ironsi's government rapidly lost support, and another military group took over on July 29, 1966. A young officer named Yakubu Gowon (considered a neutral) soon became head of the Federal Military Government (FMG), as well as Supreme Commander of the Armed Forces. Ironsi was assassinated.

Resentment built up against the Ibo. The people of the north attacked Ibo people who had settled there in large numbers. Several thousand Ibo were killed, and thousands of others fled to the east.

The new government was willing to change the constitution to calm the agitated Ibo people of the east, but Ibo leader E.O. Ojukwu, military commander of the region, insisted that the Eastern Region should be completely separate.

In order to divide the power of each of the separate regions and preserve the united country, General Gowon reorganized the four regions into twelve states —three from the Eastern Region, six from the North, and one each for Lagos, the West, and all the Midwest. This, he hoped, would also provide better representation for all ethnic groups, especially those that often had been dominated by the larger groups.

However, on May 30, 1967, Colonel Ojukwu issued a proclamation creating a Republic of Biafra from what had been the Eastern Region. He declared that Biafra had not withdrawn from the Federal Republic but had been expelled.

Fighting broke out on July 6, and the Federal troops soon took over much of the northern part of Biafra. Less than a year later the Biafran territory had been reduced to a quarter of its original size as Port Harcourt, Calabar, and Enugu were captured by Federal troops.

Even Nigerians in very small, remote villages have felt the effects of Western technology—as is demonstrated by the electric street lights of the village shown here.

This young refugee and his mother are waiting for their ration of food as part of the Biafran relief program.

A long period in which neither side could gain victory was followed by a drive of the FMG forces from the south. This broke the Biafran defenses. Ojukwu fled into exile and a surrender was signed at Lagos on January 15, 1970, ending thirty terrible months of civil war.

YAKUBU GOWON

The bitter struggle between Biafra and the FMG focused world attention on this previously little-known region of the world, especially on the young leader who was so determined to hold his country together.

The many successes of Yakubu (Jack) Gowon as leader of his nation gave him international prominence as an influential figure in both African and world affairs. His success in bringing about recovery in the Ibo areas and healing the wounds of war paved the way for his country to make many changes. His creation of twelve states from the four regions has been called even more important than winning the war. It helped to break up the power of rival groups and keep the various forces in balance.

Nigeria's rich mineral and agricultural resources are being used both at home and abroad. Many new all-weather roads, piped water, dams, factories, government offices, schools, hospitals, and universities have also been built.

Zambia, Gabon, Tanzania, and the Ivory Coast had recognized Biafran independence. After the war, General Gowon moved to restore normal relations with them, improve relations with all African nations, and give important financial aid to Nigeria's neighbors. Gowon also served as head of the Organization of African Unity, and Nigeria may become the leader in a possible new federation with some of its neighbors.

This remarkable man belongs to the small Anga group from northern Nigeria. His father, Yohanna, was an evangelist for the Church Missionary Society, and the son's philosophy of government is said to reflect his early Christian training. When Ojukwu mocked him as a "Bible-toting softy," Gowon replied that "the demands of statesmanship today are such that lessons of both the battlefield and of the church are essential."

Gowon attended officer training school in Ghana, then went to the Royal Military College in England. There he developed great respect for Britain's military and democratic traditions. He became the leader of his nation while still in his thirties.

OVERTHROW

In spite of his many accomplishments, however, Head of State Gowon seemed unable to cure many of his country's ills. One of the worst of these is the corruption of officials at almost every level of government. Gowon himself seemed almost alone in being considered completely honest and incorruptible. He does not drink, smoke, or swear, and while in office he shunned all forms of personal extravagance. He and his wife and family did not live in a huge official mansion and avoided great and expensive pomp and ceremony.

Nevertheless, there was growing anger among his countrymen about Gowon's inability to keep the military governors of the states and large numbers of army officers from making themselves wealthy at the country's expense.

Also, annual inflation ranged from 30 to 80 percent, taking a terrible financial toll among people whose average income was no higher than $150 per year. Students and intellectuals were also afraid the head of state would fail to keep his promise to return the country's government to elected officials in 1976.

When the government gave civil servants a pay raise of 133 percent, there were widespread strikes and dissatisfaction. Walkouts among public-service workers left the country without adequate water pressure or electric power, sometimes for weeks at a time.

Consequently, it probably came as no surprise to Head of State Gowon to hear that he had been overthrown. Word of the coup came to him as he attended the meeting of the Organization of African Unity in Kampala, Uganda, in early August 1975. Colonel Namvan Garba, commander of Gowon's own elite bodyguard, went on Lagos radio to announce the head of state's overthrow. There was no bloodshed or widespread strife.

The former head of state took the news calmly. He already had sent his family to England, and he joined them there in exile, although the new government said he was free to return without fear of any consequences.

Gowon's successor was Brigadier General Murtala Ramat Mohammed, like Gowon a graduate of Sandhurst military school in England. Mohammed had been one of the principal planners of the coup in 1966 that put General Gowon in office. In addition he was a military hero of the war against Biafra.

Mohammed quickly moved to cut down

In the past only boys studied the Muslim holy book as part of their Islamic religious education; today both boys and girls study the Koran.

corruption by removing almost every high official from power, including provincial governors, cabinet members, and army commanders.

However, in spite of widespread personal popularity and considerable success in reforming the government and cutting down inflation, Mohammed also had his problems. He was a Fulani, and many felt he would favor the Hausa-Fulani peoples of the north. The 1976 census had indicated that the Hausa-Fulani were even more numerous and powerful than anyone had supposed. There was fear that the old rivalries among the north, south, and east might break out again. Also, there was growing distrust of certain of Mohammed's political moves that favored leftist causes.

On Friday, February 13, 1976, a group of military men led by Lieutenant Colonel Musa Dimka ambushed and gunned down Head of State Mohammed as he was being driven to his office in the Dodan barracks headquarters. The government put down the revolt quickly, with a loss of about thirty lives, and Olasegun Obasanjo was selected by the ruling council to replace Mohammed.

Nigeria went into seven days of mourning for its assassinated chief. No one could forecast the future of this great and wealthy land with any certainty. Later in 1976 the military rulers formed a forty-nine-member panel to draw up a new constitution that provides for Nigeria's return to democratic rule by 1979. The first elections for local government councils were held in December 1976, and conferences on the new constitution were held in 1977.

GOVERNMENT

The FMG's Suspension and Modification Decree of March 1967 changed many important sections of the previous constitution and gave formal recognition to the military government. The principal policy-making body became the twenty-two-member Supreme Military Council. The twenty-one-member Federal Executive Council was composed mostly of civilians, forming a kind of cabinet. As chairman of both councils, the leader's official title was Head of State. Since there was no parliament, the FMG ruled by decree.

Except for the fact that they cannot review the military government's decrees, the structure of the courts is changed little from the earlier constitution. The Federal Supreme Court at Lagos has jurisdiction for both original and appeals cases. It has a Chief Justice and five judges.

In 1976 the twelve states were divided once again, into nineteen states. Each of the states has a High Court of Justice which hears both original cases and appeals cases from lower-level courts. Each state also has a governor who appoints civilian commissioners who manage the various state ministries. Each state is represented in the Supreme Military Council. A

new constitution might bring changes in the structure of state governments.

EDUCATION

Compared to other African countries, Nigeria has a high proportion of university graduates. However, in 1975, 75 percent of the people could not read or write. Five years before that, 90 percent were illiterate. Education is growing very rapidly in Nigeria.

A type of formal education in what is now Nigeria began in the north centuries ago. A small and select number of Muslim boys were permitted to study the Koran, the Muslim holy book, and learn to read and write Arabic script. At their peak, about 1913, there were 19,000 Koranic schools in Nigeria with about 135,000 students.

"Western" education arrived with the Christian missionaries in the mid-1800s, although some attempts had been made in education by early Portuguese visitors. The first mission school was founded at Badagri in 1842. Fifty more mission schools were established within less than twenty years. Missionary teachers followed methods similar to those used in England.

In 1877 the British government began giving money to support mission schools in the Lagos colony. Not until 1899, however, did the government establish any schools of its own.

The first secondary school, King's

Sokoto

SOKOTO

Kano

KANO

BORNO

Maiduguri

KADUNA

Kaduna

BAUCHI

Bauchi

Jos

NIGER

Minna

Abuja
FEDERAL CAPITAL
TERRITORY

PLATEAU

Yola

OYO

Ilorin

KWARA

GONGOLA

Abeokuta
Ibadan
OGUN
ONDO
Akure

Ikeja

LAGOS

Makurdi

BENUE

Enugu

Benin
City

ANAMBRA

BENDEL

IMO

Owerri

CROSS-
RIVER

RIVERS

Port
Harcourt

Calabar

NIGERIA
STATES

College, was founded in 1909. It, too, followed the British system, and only boys were allowed to attend. Most of the graduates of King's College went into the civil service.

As late as 1945, 99 percent of Nigeria's schools were operated by religious groups, though most were assisted and regulated by the government. The regional governments began to plan for free, universal, compulsory primary education in about 1952. This meant that every child would be required to attend school; but there was not enough money for that. So in various areas the "free" or the "compulsory" requirement was dropped. Problems also occurred because there were still not enough secondary schools (most are residential schools), some schools did not teach the skills Nigeria needed most, and many rural children dropped out of school early.

During the civil war, schools were completely closed in the war region.

Though English is the official national language, in recent years classes have been conducted until the third or fourth year in whatever local language is widely used. Secondary-school classes are taught in English, and students must pass an entrance exam to be eligible to attend.

Today about three and a quarter million students attend 16,530 primary and secondary schools in Nigeria. They study such subjects as arithmetic, writing, reading, natural science, religion, history, geography, drawing, handcrafts, health science, English, and local languages. In 1977 the government embarked on a program that would ensure every Nigerian child at least a primary education.

The secondary schools grant the West African School Certificate after five years and a special exam. The West African Higher School Certificate exam is taken by students who want to go on to a university.

The first institution of higher education in Nigeria was the University College at Ibadan, founded in 1948. In 1962 it became the University of Ibadan. It was the first Nigerian university to offer study for advanced degrees.

The University of Nigeria was opened at Nsukka in 1960, and the University of Lagos was established in 1962. It is operated by the federal government. In the north, at Zaria, is Ahmadu Bello University, named for the man who was premier of the Northern Region until his assassination in January 1966. With 14,000 students it is the largest university in black Africa. It opened in 1962. Bayero University College at Kano, which offers courses in Islamic studies, was a branch of Ahmadu Bello University until the mid-1970s.

The University of Ife opened in 1961 and two years later the Institute of African Studies at this university was opened. The Institute has attracted scholars from all over the world.

Six more universities—at Kano, Maiduguri, Port Harcourt, Sokoto, Jos, and Ilorin—were opened in 1975 and 1976. Over 40,000 Nigerian students are enrolled in the country's universities. Many other Nigerians study at colleges and universities all over the world.

Natural Treasures

MINERAL RICHES

The particular day that this particular event happened in 1956 is not even recorded in most histories of Nigeria, and yet it was to become of great importance to that country as well as the rest of the energy-hungry world.

A German firm had been scouring the area for oil from as early as 1908 until the beginning of World War I. Shell-British Petroleum took up the hunt again in 1938 and intensified its exploration in 1946. However, it was not until ten years later that the much-sought wealth actually was found at Oloibiri in the Niger delta.

Today the entire delta and much of the offshore region is dotted with oil fields and producing wells, and Nigeria has become one of the world's major petroleum powers. Experts feel that oil may be discovered in many other areas of the country as well, even more firmly entrenching the region as one of the world's greatest sources of petroleum and natural gas.

Coal was first discovered in the Enugu area in 1909, and the first mines opened in 1915. Vast coal reserves are known to exist in the Enugu area, and even larger ones elsewhere in the central part of the country. Coal can probably be located in many other areas, but because oil is easier to use, new veins of coal have not been searched out very extensively yet. Nigeria does have large deposits of lignite.

Tin has probably been used in the region since prehistoric times. For centuries it has been processed in smelters oper-

A worker taps a palm tree for its oil. Palm oil is one of Nigeria's most valuable resources.
MINISTRY OF INFORMATION

51

ated by the Hausa. Nigeria is one of the world's great sources of that invaluable metal, and it is likely that new tin reserves will continue to be found for some time.

Very large deposits of a rather poor quality iron ore have long been known. In cooperation with the Soviet Union, the government is setting up a huge new iron-steel complex. Expanding exploration will also probably result in additional important iron discoveries.

Related to iron by use are the plentiful reserves of columbite—probably the largest reserves in the world of this rare metal. This important mineral is used in producing heat-resistant steel products for jet engines, gas turbines, and similar high-heat generators. Most columbite and some tantalite are found in the same areas as is the tin ore.

Deposits of lead and zinc, with some silver, extend for a distance of 350 miles in the area of Abakaliki and Zurak and some parts of the northeast. The deposits of limestone are widely separated, with important formations in the lower basin of the Gongola River, near Enugu, in Bendel and Sokoto states, and near the city of Lokoja.

Other minerals found include monazite, thorite, and zircon as by-products of tin mining, as well as alluvial gold, wolframite, and kaolin. At the present time many other minerals have been classified as "minor" (not found in abundance). These include rutile, mica, topaz, diatomite, asbes-

The search for oil continues as petroleum becomes more and more valuable as an export.

52

Workers at an Ibadan sawmill convert huge trees into lumber that will find many uses in countries around the world.

tos, gypsum, beryl, fluorite, ilimenite, graphite, bismuth, and copper.

FIELD AND FOREST

Although as much as a third of the total land area is tree-covered, almost 90 percent of Nigeria's commercial timber grows in the high forest areas of the west, midwest, and southeast. The valuable mangrove is found in only about 85 square miles of swampland. Northern savanna woodland includes nearly 29,000 square miles and the southern high forests cover

about 7,500 square miles.

More than a hundred species of trees growing in Nigeria can be used commercially. Tropical hardwoods include species with such exotic names as agba, afzelia, mansonia, and sapele.

The government has a program underway for intensive planting of pines and testing of other trees. In Nigeria's tropical climate, some varieties of trees grow more quickly than they would in their native areas.

By far the most valuable trees in Nigeria are the cocoa trees and oil palms. Historically, perhaps, more of the people have depended on these trees for their livelihood than on any other resource. Oil palms yield both fruit and oil. Nearly a million and a half acres of cocoa trees are being cultivated in the country.

WILDLIFE

Since Nigeria is in a tropical area, most of the large and exotic animals of Africa are to be found there, though not in the larger numbers sometimes found elsewhere. Among the rarest are the gorillas of the high-forest region. Chimpanzees, drill baboons, and a variety of monkeys also may be found there. And although most people do not think of this as the land of the elephant, those great animals can be found in some of the forest areas. Dwarf antelopes and wild hogs, usually seen in zoos, also live in the Nigerian wilds.

Nigeria is not without the king of animals; lions are fairly abundant. The increasingly rare cheetah may still be found in the savanna areas, as well as jackals, hyenas, and other predators. Another distinctive animal, found in rapidly decreasing numbers, is the Nigerian giraffe, also a savanna resident. The northern savannas are home to the fascinating scimitar-horned oryx as well as a variety of gazelles.

What tropical African country would be complete without the hippopotamus? These ponderous animals are found along the Niger and Benue rivers, as are the strange freshwater manatee and the sinister crocodile. Among the other reptiles, the largest are the African and royal pythons.

These unusual fish, caught in Nigerian waters, are displayed at an agricultural fair.

Poisonous varieties include the black cobra, green mamba, and giant viper. Lizards and chameleons live almost everywhere. Tortoises are a favorite creature in Nigerian folk tales, for they are thought to be "wise and unconquerable."

Among the birds, no African land should be without the largest of all, and Nigeria indeed can boast of its ostriches. Other bird life of the country is extremely varied. The strange plantain-eating touracos, multi-hued parrots, and awkward hornbills are just three of Nigeria's fascinating birds. Great flocks of flamingo, marabou, and ibis live in the north, where the bustard also may be found. Other wading fowl include the herons and storks. Elsewhere, guinea and ground fowl provide contrast to the soaring eagles and equally sharp-eyed kingfishers.

Some of the world's most interesting insect life may be found in Nigeria. These include the goliath beetles, which may grow to five inches in length and must rank among the world's largest insects. The male is often seen moving along while carrying his mate clutched between his huge mandibles. Many types of butterflies and moths in the forest region also are noted for their large size and great numbers. Among other insects which unfortunately grow to large size in Nigeria are some varieties of the poisonous scorpion.

Other distasteful insects include the mosquito and the most dreaded and destructive of them all—the tsetse fly.

River fish include the catfish, carp, and shrimp, as well as the Nile perch and tilapia. Common coastal fish include mackerel, bream, sardine, threadfin, and croaker. Sharks, tarpon, barracuda, and rays are also found. Among the commercial fish are the shrimp or prawns found in fishing grounds off the Niger delta.

Unrestricted hunting has reduced the numbers of much of the larger wildlife, and the spread of human population threatens other species. The first game reserve, the Yankari, was not set up until 1957. It lies about 40 miles southeast of Bauchi and covers about 840 square miles. The Borgu Game Reserve was established in 1962. It covers 1,500 square miles west of Kainji Lake.

The People Live in Nigeria

DIVERSE MILLIONS

The most important facts about the people of Nigeria might be their number and their diversity.

Estimates of the total population range from sixty to seventy million. Even the lowest estimates give Nigeria twice the population of any other African nation. In fact, Nigeria's people encompass more than one-sixth of the entire population of the continent, and the country ranks somewhere between tenth and twelfth among all the countries of the world in population.

Within this vast number of people is an equally staggering variety of peoples. There are at least 250 language or ethnic groups, speaking more than 400 languages or dialects. The Nigerian Ministry of Information lists nine main ethnic groups, each with a population of over one million. The largest of these is the Hausa, with nearly twelve million people. Almost as numerous are the Yoruba, with about eleven and a half million. They are followed by the Ibo with ten million and the much smaller Fulani (Fulbe), Kanuri, Ibibio, Tiv, Ijaw, and Edo.

Nigeria's official language is English, but nearly everyone in Nigeria speaks at least two languages. One is always the language of the individual's particular ethnic group. Others might be English, the official national language, and also the common language of the region in which the individual lives. In the north, Hausa is the

This young couple is from northern Nigeria. They will have many more opportunities to learn about the world than their parents had.

lingua franca (common language) while Yoruba is spoken in the west and Ibo in the east. Within these three general geographic divisions there are nine specific language divisions.

The differences between Nigeria's north and south, east and west were considered by many to be so great that no single nation ever could be formed that would unite them. Care was taken to create the state boundaries so that no ethnic group would feel it was being discriminated against. Differences are still present, but since the civil war, most of the people seem to have decided that it is better to get along together. They appear to realize that the various parts of the country are dependent on one another in many ways, and that it is in the best interests of everyone to unify the nation.

LIVING STANDARDS

The ways in which the people live are as diverse as the people themselves. Mud and wattle or adobe brick walls with corrugated metal or thatched roofs contrast with modern apartments and bungalows. The population density of the country is already greater than that of the United States.

In many parts of the country, parents, children, aunts, uncles, cousins, and grandparents live in *compounds*. This is the traditional way of life throughout much of rural Africa. The number of individual houses within the compound depends on the size of the family. Cooking is often done in a common yard. Compounds sometimes have as many as a thousand residents, all of whom are members of a particular *lineage*. Lineage, or descent from a common ancestor, is the structure on which much of traditional ethnic society is based in Nigeria.

Rapidly increasing numbers of the younger people are now deserting the traditional ways and flocking to the cities. In the last few years Lagos has passed Ibadan as the nation's largest city and has been growing at the incredible rate of 20 percent per year.

The new emigrants think that life will be better for them in the city. But many of them find they must live in quickly put-up packing-crate shanties. Thousands of these sprawl out over the countryside. Lagos itself is built on a series of islands; this neatly isolates the heart of the city from its rapidly growing suburbs.

The rapid and uncontrolled growth of Lagos has led some of its people to say that it is ungovernable. In the spring of 1976, the official capital was moved to Abuja, which is exactly in the geographical center of Nigeria. However, a city must first be built at this location, and work began on it shortly after the announcement was made. Until Abuja is ready, the goverment will still be administered from Lagos.

Both the government and the people are working to improve the country's standard of living. For example, nearly a billion dollars already has been spent on workers' housing.

The thatched hut (above) and the modern skyscrapers (below) provide striking examples of the different ways of life followed by Nigeria's people.

The Ibo people, although defeated in the war, are leaders in seeking to improve the conditions of living. There is an important phrase in the Ibo language that means "getting up," or improving one's position in life. The immense energy and ambition of the Ibo, and their long traditions of cooperation, have helped to inspire many of their countrymen in "getting up."

Typical of the cooperative efforts are such groups as the Ibo Improvement Unions. These organizations regularly make contributions to building funds for schools and hospitals, provide scholarship and travel funds, and otherwise help both the individual and the group.

Members of the Esusu organizations of the Yoruba regularly contribute an agreed amount to the general treasury. At each meeting the entire amount is given to one of the members in rotation. This sum provides for increased savings, for certain luxuries, or for trading. It also builds up friendships among the members.

Yoruba women who sell their goods at the market have a remarkable reputation for their great business ability. For generations they have had strong unions to control the supply and price of goods sold, to keep down bickering and competition among themselves, and to provide social situations.

Many cooperatives have evolved that are not based on ethnic groups. One women's weaving cooperative has more than 80,000 members, operates a clinic for children, and conducts literacy (reading and writing) classes for women.

HEALTH AND WELFARE

Much of Nigeria's vast oil income is being used to aid the general growth of the country. Many health and welfare programs are administered by the individual states. They receive part of the money for these programs from the federal treasury.

On the national level, workers' compensation, social security, sickness and maternity compensation, medical benefits, and other programs are well established, along with many voluntary retirement and insurance programs. The Social Welfare Division has provided such social services as juvenile courts, day-care centers, the rehabilitation of delinquents, community centers, and organizations for adult literacy and education, as well as the organization of voluntary services. Other welfare activities are largely carried on by the various religious groups.

The government created the Second National Development Plan for the years 1970-1974 so it could plan how best to spend its money for the good of the nation during those five years. It has alloted more than $1.5 billion for the development of health programs. These programs are particularly helpful to people who work for the government, or for a large company, though efforts are made to reach as many rural Nigerians as possible.

The annual birth rate in Nigeria is 59.6 per thousand people with the death rate at 24.9 per thousand. So the population is obviously increasing very rapidly. This rapid increase is most evident in the large

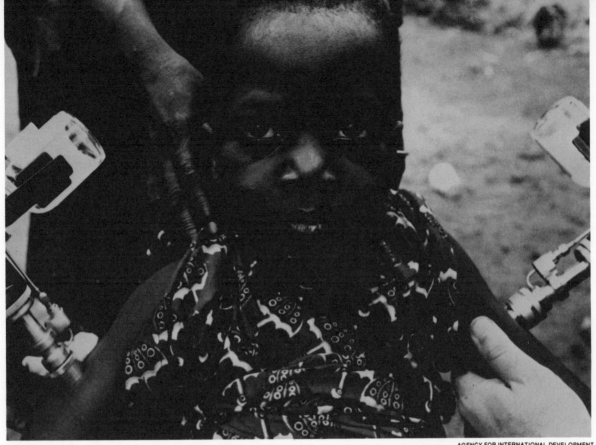

This young Nigerian remains surprisingly calm while getting two inoculations at once! The inoculations are part of a government program of disease prevention. Medical personnel visit cities, towns, and remote villages to provide health care.

cities, which are becoming very overcrowded and in which many people live in very poor housing.

The average life expectancy is fifty years. The many deaths from diseases like tuberculosis, leprosy, malaria, measles, and respiratory diseases like pneumonia—as well as the high rate of infant deaths—keep the average life expectancy low. There is only one hospital bed for each 1,782 inhabitants and only one physician for every 36,500 people. The severe shortage of doctors, nurses, medical assistants, and technologists causes many problems. The government is making strong efforts to train more people in these careers. Modern medicine has been brought to the countryside by religious missionary groups and mobile health units operated by the government. Even so, many people still do not trust modern doctors and prefer the traditional treatments they receive from local practitioners. The local practitioners add magic to their medicine, for much of Nigeria's population still believes that disease is caused by supernatural powers.

Local traditional doctors fall into two main categories—witch doctors and herbalists. Many medications used by the herbalists are known in Western science to be effective. Unfortunately, some of them can cause great harm, such as the bush tea. It can induce a fatal liver disease in one-third of the people who take it.

To the north, the *mallam* (Koranic scholars and teachers) are the traditional doctors.

RELIGION

About 50 percent of the people follow the Islamic faith, and in addition a large number of people are Christians. There are also many small religious groups scattered throughout the country.

Islam is predominant in the "Holy North," but there are considerable numbers of Muslims (the name for believers in Islam) in other parts of the country, and the faith is growing on a nationwide basis. Islam is based on a belief that a man named Muhammad, who lived in the Arabian city of Mecca about fourteen centuries ago, is a prophet of God, or Allah. Allah revealed to Muhammad a text called the Koran, which is the holy book of Islam. Faithful Muslims follow the Five Pillars of Islam, which include a statement of faith, regular prayer, giving money to the poor, fasting during the daylight hours of the Islamic month of Ramadan, and making a pilgrimage to Mecca. The religion came to Nigeria from the northwestern countries of Africa, where it is very strong.

Christianity first arrived in Nigeria by way of the coast, where European missionaries were first able to work. Gradually the missionaries and their new religion penetrated inland. Today more than half of the Ibibio people are Christians; nearly half the Ibo and a somewhat smaller proportion of the Yoruba are also members of this faith. These three groups make up the majority of the Nigerian Christians, but the religion is found throughout the peoples of Nigeria. The Anglican church (Church of England) is the largest Christian denomination, but most other denominations are active in the country.

In some parts of Nigeria both Muslim and Christian faiths have been modified by the traditional religious beliefs. These old beliefs still flourish in some areas.

People in many rural areas of the country, particularly in southern Borno state and in Benue and Plateau states, still hold to their traditional religions. These usually include a system of many gods and spirits, as well as some form of ancestor worship. In general the traditional belief is in one major god, below whom are a large number of lesser gods. Below them are several classes of spirits who are believed to be found around the countryside. On the lowest level are the spirits of the ancestors. Each ethnic group has its own ways to communicate with its gods and spirits, but every traditional religion includes cult groups, groups led by professional or volunteer priests that direct much of their worship to one particular spirit or deity.

SOCIAL CLASS

Nearly every ethnic group in Nigeria had a strict traditional structure of social class or status. Each person knew who his superiors were and who his inferiors were. Yet there were ways in which a person could move up or down in status. The basic structure within most groups was the lineage, or clan. A lineage might have thousands of members, but each member is a descendant of (or married to a descendant of) one person.

Among the Yoruba, wealth was very important. Wealth could enable a man to become one of the palace chiefs, a group of men directly responsible to the king. Wealth could also enable a man to move upward within his own lineage by purchasing privileges and ranks to which his lineage was entitled.

The Hausa-Fulani of the north hold a person's occupation as a measure of status. Rulers (kings or emirs) are at the top of this scale, while butchers are near the bottom. Traditionally, there has been very little mobility in this society, since most sons take up their father's occupation. However, people who work in business and industry have many options for change. Faithfulness and piety in the Muslim religion is also an important measure of status among these northern groups.

There is not such a defined system of class among the Ibo. In their traditional society, each individual, family, or village must prove itself worthy of status. But it is very important to attain high status, for the Ibo believe one's status remains in a life after death. As with the Yoruba, status can be "purchased," though not in the same way. Wealthy Ibo must own a beautiful country house, send their children through school, and contribute to the development of their towns. High-status towns are those with large or unique facilities such as a huge market, running water, or electricity.

MARRIAGE AND FAMILY

There are two forms of marriage in Nigeria. In the south, in the cities, *monogamous* (one husband-one wife) Christian marriages are found. Traditionally, marriages have been *polygamous* (one husband-many wives) and included a payment called *bridewealth* made by the husband to the bride's family for rights to her children and her productivity. In the "Holy North," Muslims limit their polygamy to four wives for each husband.

The idea of monogamy was brought to the country by European Christian missionaries, and many Nigerians still resent it. They also brought the ideas of choosing one's marriage partner rather than having the marriage arranged by parents. Divorce is possible throughout the country, and in the north the divorce rate is quite high. The partner "at fault" in a divorce is required to pay back the bridewealth. Traditional marriages are made for the purpose of having children, and there is far more closeness between child and parent than there is between husband and wife. Even those couples who have met and married in the city, far away from their families, usually plan to return to the home village after retirement.

In polygamous marriages, the first wife is usually the leader among the wives. Frequently she is the only one for whom a full bridewealth has been paid. Age is very important in relations among wives. When the wives are close together in age there is frequently more conflict than when the senior wife is much older.

The men of nearly every ethnic group in Nigeria observe the custom of the *special friend.* These friendships begin in boyhood and last throughout life. Men usually feel closer to their special friends than they do to their own families. Special friendships among Nigerian Muslims are not as close, but the special friend is often allowed into areas of the house usually reserved for the family.

SHARO

When boys and girls in traditional Africa are about to become men and women, frequently they must undergo initiation rites and ceremonies. Each ethnic group has its own version of these rites, and sometimes they can be very brutal. An example of this in Nigeria is the *sharo,* a practice of the Fulani people of the north. It has been illegal for over twenty years but is still practiced sometimes in remote regions. The sharo is performed by two boys, usually best friends. Each in turn

must flog the other three times with a large stick. The boy being flogged cannot show that he is feeling any pain, or he will be disgraced before the girls of the village and will not be able to marry. The ceremony was outlawed because very brutal, even fatal, blows are frequently administered. Yet some Fulani still practice this rite in secret.

Most ethnic initiation rites are much less painful. Some extend over many days or weeks. Often boys or girls undergoing the rites are taken into the forest away from the rest of the village.

MUSIC

Music, especially singing, has always been very important to the peoples of Nigeria. Songs were sung for nearly every occasion, by individuals or choruses. Some people, such as the northern Muslims, had full-time musicians who were organized into guilds. In most other groups, the musicians did not perform full time.

Musicians could choose from a greater variety of musical instruments in the north. Southern instruments included the raft zither, the thumb piano, metal gongs, cymbals, rattles, wind instruments, and drums. In the north some of the instruments were more complicated, such as the brass trumpet called the *kakaki.* Musicians there also play a stringed instrument with three or four strings called the *molo* and a reed flute called the *algaita.*

When radio came to Nigeria in the

Music, played on a traditional instrument (left) or as the accompaniment to an ethnic dance (below), is a basic and important part of Nigeria's cultural heritage.

This statue is one example of the beauty of modern Nigerian art.

1930s, the people had their first major exposure to Western music. However, Western music had been in the country on a very small scale since the late nineteenth century.

In the 1950s and 1960s a combination of Western and African popular music emerged. It was known as *highlife* music, and it became very popular throughout black Africa.

Some composers, most of whom teach at Nigerian schools and universities, have written in both Western and African classical music forms. Several have combined both forms to produce compositions for religious services and stringed instruments.

One of the most interesting modern composers of music is Lazarus Edweme. He works to merge African and Western classical music traditions into his string compositions and religious masses. Although none of the composers are internationally famous, other composers of Western-style classical music include Ayo Bankole, Akin Euba, and Fela Sowande.

ART

The cultural tradition of Nigeria extends back for centuries before the time of the cast bronzes and pottery of Ife. These were made up to eight hundred years ago, yet some still have not been surpassed even today. Nigeria has also long had a tradition of beautiful sculpture. One of the best-known modern wood sculptors is Lamidi Fakeye, founder of the Nigerian

Artisans prepare pieces to sell at their village market.

Society of Professional Artists. Jacob Afolabi is known for his relief sculpture in large concrete structures. Among the most prominent sculptors is Ben Osawe, who works in bronze, clay, stone, and wood, particularly ebony. Erhabor Emokapae is a painter as well as a sculptor.

The opening of a cultural center at Oshogbo in 1964 attracted a number of fine young artists to that city. One of the better known of these is Muraina Oyelami, who started with an abstract style but changed to more realistic work such as his famous *Dead Bodies,* portraying the civil war. Other prominent members of the Oshogbo school are Jimoh Buraimoh and Twins Seven Seven. The latter, who is famous for his painting and collages, took this nickname because it reflects his exact birth position within his family.

One of the better-known Lagos artists, Uche Okeke, uses modern art forms to interpret spirits and other mythical creatures. Others who work in Lagos are Jimo Akolo and Ben Enwonwu.

In 1977 the International Festival of Black Arts and Culture was held at Lagos. Artists from all over the world traveled to Nigeria to exhibit their works. They, as well as many visitors, also had the opportunity to learn about the works of the Nigerian artists.

LITERATURE

Because of the lack of a written language, especially in the south, history and literature in Nigeria were passed orally from person to person. Often historical sagas and long chants were performed as dramatic productions. Parents told their children folk tales, proverbs, and riddles and the historic traditions were thus kept alive. In parts of the north the written Arabic language was available, but was known only to a very few people.

After the Europeans arrived, a number of local languages began to be written down in the Roman alphabet. Some modern Nigerian poets use the traditional languages in their work. Among these one of the best known is Ikponmwosa Osemwegie, who has preserved many songs, poems, and sacred myths in *Poems in Bini*.

The first literary works in English were on historical or political subjects. Nnamdi Azikiwe, who later became prime minister, published two books on African politics in the 1930s, and a two-volume autobiography in the 1970s. In the 1940s short stories issued in pamphlets began to be published. Many of these stories were taken from the folk tales of Nigeria's various ethnic groups. Cyprian Ekwensi and Amos Tutuola were two of the better-known short-story writers. Ekwensi later published a novel called *People of the City*. Appearing in 1954, it was the first Nigerian novel to be written in English and the first Nigerian literature of any kind to be published outside Africa.

As Nigerian literature expanded during the 1960s, the Ibo writer Chinua Achebe came to be considered the foremost novelist of the country. Younger novelists now include Elechi Amadi, Onuora Nxebwu, Jon Munoye, and Flora Nwapa. Nwapa's novel *Effrru* was the first in English to be published by a Nigerian woman.

The People Work in Nigeria

How does a poor, neglected country almost overnight become a powerful and influential member of the international community? The answer, of course, is to strike it rich. And that is just what Nigeria did. Within the amazing space of less than ten years Nigeria rose from a "nobody" in the petroleum industry to rank sixth among all the petroleum-producing nations of the world.

It helps, too, to have the world's wealthiest nation as your best customer. With the exception of Canada, the United States buys more oil from Nigeria than any other nation. And of course energy has become the world's greatest need and the most important economic concern.

The wealth pouring into the country from oil would appear to be only at its beginning, since many experts are convinced that the known sources of petroleum are only a small part of what will be found eventually. All of Nigeria is affected by this sudden increase in export income. Parts of the country have come to resemble the "boom towns" of the American gold rush in the mid-nineteenth century. Even greater wealth would be available almost at once if Nigeria could find some means of using the great natural gas supplies which now must be burned because they cannot be used or stored. More than two billion cubic feet of natural gas are wasted each day by "flaring."

Much other wealth could be realized from the mineral resources of Nigeria. However, these have not been developed to the extent that petroleum has, since oil brings the quickest and easiest return.

Coal has long been mined, but it is generally too costly in comparison with petroleum. Cheaper means must be found to

Petroleum is truly "liquid gold" to Nigeria. Its discovery has provided a tremendous boost to the country's economy.

mine and transport the large coal supplies.

In tin production, Nigeria ranks first on the African continent, but the total amount it supplies to the world market is relatively low. However, tin probably ranks next to petroleum as a source of mineral income for the country.

In one rare and unusual metal, Nigeria ranks first in the world. This mineral is columbite. However, cheaper substitutes are being found for this mineral, which helps steel resist heat, and the importance of columbite as a source of income is diminishing. Tantalite is another plentiful mineral in Nigeria that is also diminishing in economic importance.

Altogether, Nigeria's rich mineral resources produce more than 70 percent of the nation's total domestic income, and this percentage appears to be increasing because of oil.

FARM AND FOREST

Before the coming of oil riches, Nigeria was almost entirely an agricultural country. Unlike some of the other large countries of Africa, Nigeria is blessed with an abundance of good farmland. It produces so much food in such variety that it not only sustains the largest population on the continent but also sells much of its foods in world markets. Still more of Nigeria's crops provide raw materials for manufacturing.

Over the years, Nigeria has ranked either first or second in the world in three very important products: cocoa; kernels of the oil palm; and, most important, protein-rich peanuts (known there as groundnuts).

Most Americans think of Liberia and its famous Firestone plantation as the center of African rubber production. In reality, it is Nigeria that is the continent's leading producer of that valuable product.

Although Nigeria is experiencing a rush of people to the cities, between 70 and 80 percent of the people still work on the land. By far the largest part of Nigeria's agriculture is of the type known as *subsistence farming*. Small individual farms produce most of the needs of a family or cluster of families. However, except to the north, even many of these small farms produce more than they need for the families' own use. Each year they market some of what they grow.

Though Nigerian land can produce almost any kind of nourishment, the people's diet has not often been a balanced one. The greatest lack is in protein-rich foods. At Nigeria's Federal Institute of Industrial Research, a protein-rich food supplement has been developed which can be sold at a price most families can pay. This food is called *soy-ogi*. It is similar to the traditional Nigerian infant food called ogi, but its particular combination of corn and soya enriched with minerals provides adequate protein. Local cooks find it easy to use in their regular cooking.

Grains and livestock are the main food products of the arid northern third of the country. Its principal staple crop is a local variety of sorghum called guinea corn. Most of Nigeria's groundnuts and cotton are also grown in the north. The northern nomads raise large herds of goats, cattle, and sheep, untroubled by the deadly tsetse fly that infests much of the rest of this tropical country.

The north has far more agricultural potential than the south as far as grain crops are concerned. It may one day be known as the "breadbasket of Nigeria." Root crops, like yams, grow better in the middle belt and the south.

Because of the tsetse fly, cattle are not raised in the southern region; only a rather unimportant type of dwarf cattle can resist the terrible insect. Oxen are also subject to the tsetse fly, and the region has not been able to use these beasts of burden.

The rich tree crops are concentrated in the southern region—cocoa, palm, rubber, and kola nuts. The region also produces many hardwoods as well as fish from the Gulf of Guinea. Long-range plans call for teaching modern fishing methods to the primitive canoe fishermen of Lake Chad's coastal banks and the Niger delta. They will also be provided with new equipment. Construction of a large modern fishing terminal at Lagos was designed to improve the shrimp industry off the delta.

Three of Nigeria's major agricultural products are cocoa (right), palm kernels (below left), which are used for their oil, and groundnuts (below right).

MINISTRY OF INFORMATION

Nigeria is the world's largest producer of rubber. Its rubber trees supply the world with the basic material for thousands of different products.

Some Nigerians earn a living selling their wares in busy village markets like this one.

MANUFACTURING

Although manufacturing makes up only about 8 percent of the total domestic production, it has been growing at the extraordinary rate of 12 percent or more per year. Much of this increase has been because more and more consumer products are being manufactured for sale in Nigeria.

Among the larger industries are cement factories, lumber and plywood mills, textile mills, and a petroleum refinery. Several foreign auto makers are establishing assembly plants in Nigeria.

Although many of the new factories are as big as they can be without losing efficiency, much of the country's industry is carried on by factories so small that they do not even get into the statistics. The government estimates that there may be as many as 900,000 rural households occupied with food processing, palm oil extraction, and the making of textiles, clothing, metal products, and such products as fiber mats.

Local crafts are still important in Nigerian marketplaces. Probably the most widespread and interesting craft is the decorating of gourds or calabashes. These are made into bowls, containers, spoons, and other useful items. Traditional designs are carved or burned on. Creating artistic calabash ware is a highly respected profession, especially among the Hausa people of the north. Many Hausa men travel from market to market with their wares. Hausa women who create calabash ware can often become quite wealthy, one of the few ways for these women to do so.

Another striking craft is the making of beaded crowns worn by traditional Yoruba leaders. These are made in a cone shape and similar ones may have been made as early as the twelfth century.

TRANSPORTATION AND COMMUNICATION

Nigeria is easy to reach from all parts of the world. Flights touch down at Lagos and Kano from major cities of Europe and the Western Hemisphere. Lagos and Port Harcourt can also be reached by passenger ship, or by the more romantic route of freighters that come from the United States, Canada, or England.

Perhaps the most surprising feature of transportation in Nigeria is the very extensive system of inland waterways. The Niger River can be navigated as far as Yelwa, and the Benue to Yola, with limited navigation as far as Garoua in Cameroon. Small boats can use the Cross River for some distance. The Katsina Ala and Gongola tributaries of the Benue also are used for navigation.

The most historic of all Nigeria's waterways is the network of creeks, lagoons, and bayous that connect to form continuous water routes from the western border with Benin to the many branches of the Niger delta. These waters have carried produce and people for so long that they have become almost legendary.

AGENCY FOR INTERNATIONAL DEVELOPMENT

A Nigerian woman poles her log canoe over an inland waterway. In some areas the canoe is the fastest form of transportation.

Lagos on the western coast and Port Harcourt, located more than forty miles up the Bonny River in the eastern Niger Delta area, are Nigeria's two main ocean ports. With the ports of Calabar and Warri, these form the national system operated by the Nigerian Ports Authority. The latter two are being enlarged to relieve congestion at Lagos and Port Harcourt.

Port Harcourt is also the terminus of the main railroad line. Coal mined at Enugu is shipped to the sea on this line. There are 2,200 miles of railroads in the country.

Nigeria's railroads were built by the British. One of them makes a 28-hour journey from Lagos to Kano. From there one can return to Lagos on a 33 1/2-hour route, by way of Enugu and Port Harcourt.

Small boats or launches wander among the almost infinite number of lagoons of the coast or up the Niger River, with its innumerable delta mouths.

There are over 60,000 miles of roads in Nigeria, but little more than 10,000 miles are hard-surfaced. Major roads link Lagos with the state capitals and other large towns and ports. A well-built and well-traveled road runs from Benin and Togo to Lagos. It offers a relatively uneventful trip—except when a washout obliterates the road. Then hundreds of cars coming from Lagos face hundreds of other cars going to Lagos—across an uncompromising morass.

More venturesome land routes travel from western Cameroon or, even more exciting, from Chad. One of the world's most exciting roads plods across the Sahara from Algeria through Agades in neighboring Niger to Kano in northern Nigeria.

One of the major road problems is brought about by the Niger and Benue rivers. All principal east-west highways must cross these mighty streams. Most of the traffic is carried by ferry. In 1966 a

Work is constantly being done to build new roads and to improve existing ones in Nigeria.

UNITED NATIONS

SLOW
ROAD WORKS
AHEAD

three-lane bridge was opened between Onitsha and Asaba on the lower (southern) east-west main road. It was destroyed during the civil war but rebuilt larger by the British after the war. So far, building more bridges has not been a major priority.

There is good bus service to most parts of the country, so private driving really is not necessary. And with the relatively small number of cars in the country, traffic might be expected to be light. But the traffic of Lagos has been called "the worst in the world." Most outsiders do not have the courage to do their own driving. Behind an endless line of trucks and buses that discharge passengers every few feet, the journey by car from downtown Lagos to the international airport outside the city can require as long as four hours. In this country of possibly 70,000,000 people, there are estimated to be only 73,000 passenger cars. In the United States, with little more than three times the population, there are nearly one hundred and twenty million cars—over sixteen times as many.

All of the other modern "luxury" items —telephones, television, personal accessories—tell the same story. No matter how wealthy and ambitious, the process of development is bound to be a long one.

Enchantment of Nigeria

A FANTASTIC PLACE

Nigeria is exciting yet rugged, modern yet traditional. It is the largest nation in the world with a mostly black population, and it retains even today much of the influence of the British colonialists who occupied it for so long.

Its attractions range from Kano, one of Africa's most ancient cities of camel caravans and desert traders, to the modern skyscrapers of Lagos, the largest city between Cairo, Egypt, and Johannesburg, South Africa. Its waters are both mysterious, like the constantly changing shores and ancient reed fishing boats of Lake Chad and the maze of the Niger River delta and the coastal channels, and up-to-date, like the dams and modern ports typi-

cal of an industrialized nation. It has mills that are camel-powered and the incredible power befitting the world's sixth-largest oil exporter. It has the kingly palaces of emirs and *obas,* local traditional rulers, to the modest remodeled barracks of its constitutional chief of state.

LAGOS

Lagos is built on the island of Iddo and can only be approached by bridge or ferry, making traffic sometimes seemingly impossible to negotiate. Other islands—Ikoyi and Victoria—form part of the "suburbs" of Lagos, providing elegant locations for large and stately homes.

The port of Apapa, which can be

The city of Lagos is a modern and beautiful—but crowded—metropolis.

Victorian Beach and the other beaches of Lagos provide the people of the city with a place to enjoy themselves away from their everyday work world.

reached by ferry, or Tarkwa Beach, reached by launch, are located in the Lagos area. "Behind" Lagos (toward the mainland) is Badagry Creek.

On Iddo Island itself is beautiful Marina Drive, circling the waterfront. In the distance, is the Independence Building, one of the tallest in the country, and many other modern structures. The ultra-modern style of the City Hall contrasts greatly with the nearby Benin-style palace of the traditional *oba* (king) of Lagos.

The Nigeria Museum and the National Hall are also important buildings. However, much of Lagos is dirty and congested. New housing is being built.

One of the most fascinating attractions of Lagos is the immense public market, said by some experts to be one of the most interesting in all of Africa, a continent noted for its interesting markets. An entire section of the market is devoted to the selling of *juju*. These are the charms, potions, herbs, and other items still believed by many to have magic powers. Another large market is near the Bristol Hotel. It is one of the largest anywhere devoted entirely to the sale of textiles.

One almost wholly unexpected area of Lagos is the Brazilian area. Here live the descendants of many former slaves who returned from Brazil to Africa, bringing with them much of the South American flavor that still lingers in this section.

Local African dress is still often seen around the city. Men wear tunics of extremely bright colors over trousers which generally match, while the women wear long colorful wraparound tunics. More and more, however, the traditional costumes are being replaced by Western business suits and casual clothes such as blue jeans.

Surrounding the city, even on the outskirts, are many villages where traditional mask dances, rhythms, and shrines mix with other forms of village life. Here are found many young men and women who work in the city but return to their villages for the weekends and holidays.

YORUBALAND AND THE SOUTH

Even the larger cities not too far from Lagos have less bustle and more tradition than the capital. For years Ibadan was the largest city in Nigeria. Now Lagos has far surpassed it in population.

Ibadan is a center of Yoruba cultural life. The beautiful campus of its university houses one of the most respected English-speaking institutions in all of the con-

Rush hour in Lagos looks very much like rush hour in any large city.

MINISTRY OF INFORMATION

tinent. Plays written by African writers, including Nigeria's famous Wole Sokinka, are produced at the university, and frequently there are performances by the well-known dance or mime troupes and musical groups of the city.

Other attractions of Ibadan are the palace of the traditional ruler, or oba, and the large extended-family compounds of the city-dwelling Yoruba. Hundreds of members of a particular kinship group might live within a compound, each individual family in its own house.

Ibadan also has one of the huge cloth markets, held every sixteen days. This customary daily market becomes a colorful bazaar at night.

One of the most noted of the country's events is the series of Egungun festivals held at Ibadan from January through June. Then the hotels are crowded, and the city is proud that it has Nigeria's only truly international hotel—the Premier.

Another center of Yoruba culture is Oshogbo. It too has a famous Egungun festival, held each August. This market town is also especially noted for its forest shrines and their ancient and modern religious art. A European artist, Suzanne Wenger, was so fascinated by the local art and the religion it represented that she joined the traditional faith and became a Priestess of Oshun. Though she has been called eccentric by many critics, she serves as an important force behind the metal-

workers, masons, and other sculptors who create these unique sculptured works.

Although these monuments are rapidly filling the sacred groves of Oshogbo, the work never ceases because the faithful believe such shrines lose their sacredness if the work stops.

Artist-Priestess Wenger also built a home at Oshogbo that is one of the showplaces of the region.

The Yoruba nation was said to have been born at Ile-Ife where much of the tradition and art can be viewed in the small museum of the local *oni* (king). The huge bronze castings at Ife are said to be as fine as the more famous bronze masterpieces of historic Benin. The discovery of such works, which were made by supposedly primitive people, caused the entire world of art and archaeology to change its opinion about what the peoples who originally populated the area were like.

Some of the finest wood carvings in Africa are still being done by the modern woodcarvers whose work is sold in the street markets and finer shops of Benin.

Other interesting cities are Koko, with its canoe festival, and Onitsha, with its festival of Ofala. Another of the more intriguing annual events is the colorful fishing festival at Argungu, held in mid-February.

Oyo has long been known as a center of fine leather workers, weavers, and carvers of the beautiful decorated calabashes.

The colorful dresses worn by these Yoruba women (top) might have been made from cloth purchased at the Blue Market in Ibadan (bottom).

OTHER-WORLDLY JOS

Because the city is situated on an elevated plateau, Jos has a delightful temperate climate. Many buildings have wood-burning fireplaces, and they are much appreciated on the sometimes chilly evenings of the plateau.

This location has its disadvantages, too. It has isolated the people of the plateau area from the outside world. Even today its people show fewer influences from the outside forces that have penetrated Nigeria over the centuries.

Neither the Muslim influence in the north nor the European-Christian influence on the coast has had as much effect on the high plateau as in the rest of the country. So much of the plateau area is like going backward to an earlier and simpler time. Its people are sometimes known as the "Old People," because they inhabited the region long before the Muslim Hausa peoples and, it is thought, even before the Yoruba came to Nigeria. According to some theories, the Old People lived in the Jos area as long ago as four thousand years, to about 2000 B.C.

The animist religions and religious traditions are still very important in this region and there are a wide variety of cultures there as well.

Particularly interesting are the Kaleri peoples, who had a reputation for being fierce and warlike. Sometimes they still

The Kaleri tribesmen use masks, like this ornate one with its fierce expression, as part of their ceremonial dances.

paint their faces red with paste made from powdered laterite stone and also rub the paste into their hair to make scarlet ringlets. In addition to the famous Kaleri funeral dance, there are many others, such as the "good hunting" dance. In this dance, one of the dancers dresses in a woven sisal costume, with a sisal mask completely covering his face. His costume represents the forces of evil.

Some of the Kaleri men occasionally still pierce their noses with millet straws and wear bright circlets of beads around their heads. Most ceremonies are climaxed with a feast in which the whole community takes part, each bringing his large bowl to receive the family share of tasty stew from the general pot.

Scientists around the world were astounded in the early 1930s when archaeologists made some truly unexpected discoveries at the little village of Nok, near Jos. Among the precious items recovered were sculptures made of terra-cotta. These ranged from a few inches in size to human figures and heads that were life-sized or nearly as large as life. There was also a wide variety of animal figures in many sizes. Before these discoveries were made experts had had no knowledge that such fine cultural accomplishments had existed in this area so far back in time. In fact, authorities now believe that the Nok culture represents the first time any of the peoples of West Africa progressed into what is known as the Iron Age.

The small museum of Jos has a collection of some of the fine ceramic pieces made by the ancient Nok peoples. The museum also has examples of the crafts of the Tiv peoples and representative pieces of other art of the region.

Jos is also the center of a rich tin-mining region, and it has become a bustling city living in the present as well as in its prestigious past. For example, it has fine modern hotel accommodations as well as an excellent government-owned rest house. Yet Jos's tin industry is very, very old.

In the Jos region are many villages from which there are spectacular views of the countryside. Many people who still practice the ancient animistic faiths reside in these villages. There are also a few beautiful waterfalls in the area south of the city of Jos.

To the east of Jos, about one hundred miles away, lies the Yankari Game Reserve. It has a pleasant lodge and its star attractions are the hippos, whose natural habitat has been carefully preserved.

THE MYSTERIOUS NORTH

Kano is not only the most important city of the northern area, but also must be ranked as one of the greatest cities of ancient Africa. Although the fabled city of Timbuktu (in present-day Mali) is better known, throughout most of its history Kano has compared favorably to Timbuktu in most ways. Today, reverses of climate and economy in Timbuktu are changing it into a small, almost insignificant desert site, while Kano remains the bustling "capital" of perhaps 30,000,000 Hausa-

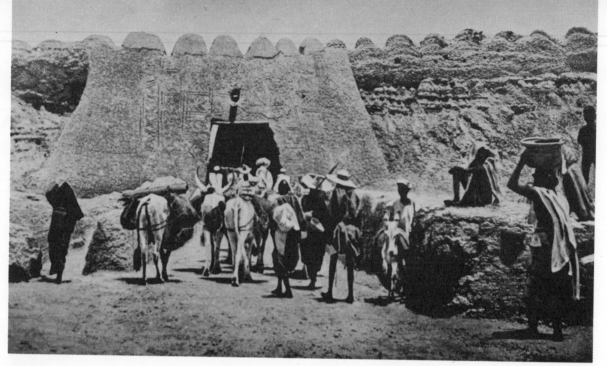

A small caravan enters one of the thirteen gates in the wall that surrounds and protects the "old city" of Kano.

speaking people who live not only in Nigeria but also in Niger, Chad, and Benin as well. For untold centuries the camel caravans have made their way across the desert to Kano from as far away as Persia (present-day Iran).

Renowned as the first major Hausa Muslim ruler was Muhammadu Rumfa. He was perhaps more responsible than anyone else for the splendor of the "old city" of Kano, which remains today much as it was in Emir Rumfu's day. The old city is still enclosed by its wall, eleven miles in circumference—built as thick as forty feet in some places. Thirteen entrances in the wall were tightly closed by sturdy and striking-looking gates encased in cowhide.

The most imposing building in the old city is the Palace of the Emirs, built more than four hundred years ago by Rumfa. Since his time, all Kano emirs have been Muslims. Although the great palace is not open to the public, sometimes an appointment can be made for a personal visit with the current emir, who still resides there.

The high dome of the palace, its twenty artistically decorated arches, and the twenty-foot high wall all add further interest. It is surrounded by a beautiful thirty-three-acre garden.

The dazzling whiteness and twin minarets of Kano's great mosque also are a principal attraction of the old city. From the minarets, one can view distant donkey and camel trains as they make their way toward the city. Also in the distance may be seen "skyscrapers" of peanuts piled as high as a four-story building, waiting to be shipped to market.

Spread out below are the houses and stores, most constructed of faded red mud with their windows no wider than slits. Many of the buildings are decorated with geometric patterns. Until 1963, non-Muslim visitors were not allowed to spend the night in the Old City without special permission. They could, however, roam to their hearts' content during the day. Today that rule no longer exists and there are even hotels inside some of the gates.

At the end of the trail for the donkey and camel trains, with their variety of wares, is the great market, where as many as 40,000 people may gather at one time. Here are found the goods of the native artisans, made in styles and by methods unchanged since ancient times. Cloth is woven by hand and dyed the deep blue that is traditional in the region. Kano craftsmen are still noted for their almost incomparable work in fine soft leathers, as well as their intricately worked silverware and jewelry. The fine work in other metals is also renowned.

Shopping at the market stalls, perhaps, will be Tuareg tribesmen just in from the Sahara, wearing turbans and caftan gowns in traditional indigo color. Making their way among the goats, sheep, donkeys, and

These workers seem very small next to the towering groundnut storage tents that surround them.
MINISTRY OF INFORMATION

UNITED NATIONS

A large part of the enchantment of Nigeria is the diversity of its ethnic groups and their lifestyles. These young men (left) bicycling on the busy streets of Lagos lead a life very different from that of the rural Fulani woman and her young child (right).

Nigeria's future lies in the hands of its people like this Hausa woman (left), this Ibo man (below left), and these young children (below right) from Anambara State.

other animals of the market will be Hausa girls bearing ceramic jars on their heads. This practice gives them a special air of grace and dignity that is further accented by the jewels they frequently wear.

An additional display of Hausa and Fulani art is found at the historic old Makama Madawaki town house, now a museum.

Kano is often said to be three cities in one. As foreign influence began to reach the area, a new town began to rise around the gates of the old. Today the "Township" portion of Kano has its fine government buildings, good department and other stores, restaurants, and other "modern" buildings and facilities.

On the outskirts, the "third" portion of Kano may be found. This is the part known before the civil war as the *sabon gari* or "new town." Here live the non-Hausa people who came to work and trade. It is a region of cheap restaurants and bars, small shops, and crowded housing.

Just outside the city itself are the buildings and campus of the bright new Bayero University College. It was formerly a branch of Ahmadu Bello University. Kano's fine airport is easily reached by direct flights from London, Rome, Khartoum, and Cairo as well as from other Nigerian cities.

At the end of the Muslim observance of Ramadan, the city puts on its great annual festival. The unbelievable riding of desert horsemen, the performances of supple acrobats, and the snake dancers are all a part of the colorful event. Everywhere visitors will be tempted by the spicy odors of roasting lamb and goats—the forerunner of the modern backyard barbecue.

There are, of couse, other cities of historic and economic importance in the north, each of them still presided over (unofficially) by their emirs or the sultan.

Sokoto is the traditional home of the sultan, who is one of several spiritual and political leaders of Muslim life in northern Nigeria. The shrines of Sokoto are visited by many thousands of pilgrims each year. The city is also the capital of the new Sokoto State.

The university town of Zaria was once the headquarters of the powerful Zazzau Emirate.

At Kaduna the old and the new mingle in the industrial and political capital of the new Kaduna State and the former North Central State. Other important northern cities are Katsina and Maiduguri.

DISSIMILARITY AND UNITY

Any visitor who manages to see each of the widely dissimilar sections of Nigeria —north, south, east, and west—comes away with a sometimes blurred impression of the nation. The groundwork has already been laid through the heritage of so many great powers and cultures of the past. And there is no mistaking the vigor in the vast population of Nigeria and a determination to make the most of the country's vast human and natural resources.

Handy Reference Section

INSTANT FACTS

Political

Official Name—Federal Republic of Nigeria

Capital—Abuja (administered from Lagos until Abuja is completed)

Form of Government—Republic, under military rule

Monetary Unit—Niara

Official Language—English

Religions—Muslim, Protestant, Catholic, Animist

Flag—Vertical stripes of green, white, and green

States	Capital
Anambra	Enugu
Bauchi	Bauchi
Bendel	Benin City
Benue	Makurdi
Borno	Maiduguri
Cross-River	Calabar
Gongola	Yola
Imo	Owerri
Kaduna	Kaduna
Kano	Kano
Kwara	Ilorin
Lagos	Ikeja
Niger	Minna
Ogun	Abeokuta
Ondo	Akure
Oyo	Ibadan
Plateau	Jos
Rivers	Port Harcourt
Sokoto	Sokoto
Federal Capital Territory	Abuja

Geographical

Area—356,699 square miles

Highest Point—Vogel Peak, 6,700 feet

Lowest Point—Sea Level
Greatest Width (east to west)—800 miles (approximately)
Greatest Length (north to south)—660 miles (approximately)

POPULATION

Total Population—70,000,000 (1977 estimate)
Population Density—165 per square mile

Population by ethnic groups (in millions) (1977 estimates)

Hausa	11.7
Yoruba	11.3
Ibo	9.3
Fulani (Fulbe)	4.8
Kanuri	2.3
Ibibio	2.0
Tiv	1.4
Ijaw	1.0
Ido	1.0

Population of principal cities (1977 estimates)

Lagos	3,000,000
Ibadan	1,200,000
Kano	700,000
Ogbomosho	45,000
Oshogbo	25,000

ECONOMY (annual figures)

Gross Domestic Product—6.8 billion
Growth Rate—12 percent

Per Capita Income—$100
Per Capita Growth Rate—9.2 percent

AGRICULTURE

Arable Land—84,000,000 acres; 30 percent cultivated
Per Capita Acres—2.1

LEGAL PUBLIC HOLIDAYS

New Year's Day, January 1
Good Friday (date varies)
Easter Monday (date varies)
National Day, October 1
Christmas Day, December 25
Boxing Day, December 26
Festival of Id-el-Fitr (date varies)
Festival of Id-el-Kabir (date varies)

YOU HAVE A DATE WITH HISTORY

c. 500 B.C.—Nok culture begins greatest development
c. 800 A.D.—Kanem civilization begins to flourish
c. 1500—Benin kingdom
c. 1600—Dutch influence begins
1750—Oyo power attains peak
1769—Mungo Park explores upper Niger River
1804—Fulani conquest begins
1830—Niger delta reached from upstream
1842—First Christian mission schools established

1861—Britain takes over Lagos

1885—Oil Rivers Protectorate formed

1886—Royal Niger Company founded

1893—Niger Coast Protectorate established

1899—First public schools established by the government

1900—Nigeria becomes an official British Protectorate

1914—Northern and southern portions united in one colony

1915—Coal mining begins

1922—Britain establishes a Nigerian constitution

1944—National Council of Nigerian Citizens (NCNC) formed

1946—Richards Constitution in force

1948—University of Ibadan founded

1954—New constitution

1956—First important commercial petroleum discovery made; Queen Elizabeth II feted during state visit

1957—First game reserve (Yankari) established

1960—Nigeria becomes sixteenth African state to achieve independence

1963—Form of government changed to Federal Republic within British Commonwealth; Institute of African Studies founded

1964—Cultural Center opens at Oshogbo

1966—Two successive military coups initiate military government

1967—Twelve states formed; Biafra proclaims independence; civil war begins

1970—Civil war ends

1975—Head of State Yakubu Gowon overthrown, July 29; Murtala Ramat Mohammed becomes Head of State

1975-76—Six new universities open

1976—Head of State Mohammed overthrown, February 13

1976—Report of Constitutional Drafting Committee, October

1976—First local elections, December

1976—Decision to move capital to Abuja announced

1976—Twelve-state system abolished; nineteen-state system created

1977—International Festival of Black Arts and Culture, Lagos, January-February

1977—National debates held on proposed constitution

Index

Page numbers in italics indicate illustration.

Abakaliki, 52
Abeokuta, 35
Abuja, 58
Achebe, Chinua, 68
Action Group, 41
Afolabi, Jacob, 67
African Studies, Institute of, 49
Agriculture, 24, 36, 53, 70, 71, *72,*
Aguiyi-Ironsi, J.T.U., 43
Airports, 75, 77, 90
Akolo, Jimo, 67
Al-Kanemi, Mohammed, 32
Amadi, Elechi, 68
Anga (people), 44
Anglican Church, 62
Animals, 54, 55
Apapa, 21, 79
Area, 9
Argungu, 83
Art, 22, 23, *23, 29, 34,* 66, *66,*
    67, 74, 75
Asaba, 77
Asika, Anthony, 8
Assob waterfall, 85
Azikiwe, Nnamdi, 41, 68

Badagri, 47
Badagry Creek, 21, 79
Balewa, Abubakar, 41, 43

Bankole, Ayo, 66
Barth, Heinrich, 36
Bauchi, 55
Bayero University College, 49,
    90
Beecroft, John, 36
Beetles, Goliath, 55
Bello, Ahmadu, 49
Bello, Ahmadu, University, 49,
    90
Bendel, 52
Benin, 9, 14, 34, 35, 75, 76,
    83, 86,
Benue River, 11, 14, 15, 18,
    36, 54, 75, 76
Benue, 62
Berlin, Conference of, 37
Biafra, 7, 8, 24, 25, 43, 44
Bilingual Center for the Train-
    ing of Museum Technicians,
    19
Birds, 55
Birth rate, 60
Blue Market (Ibadan), *82*
Bonny, 36
Bonny River, 75
Borgu Game Reserve, 55
Borno (kingdom), 32, 33
Borno (state), 62
Brazil (people), 81
Bridewealth, 63, 64

Bridges, 77
Britain (people), 35, 36, 37-41
British Commonwealth, 41
Buraimoh, Jimoh, 67

Calabar, 43, 75
Calabash carving, 22, 74, 83
Cameroon, 11, 14, 38, 75, 76
Cathay Restaurant (Lagos), 24
Chad, 11, 15, 26, 30, 31, 32,
    76, 86
Chad Basin, 12
Chad, Lake, 12, 14, 15, 71
Christianity, 26, 36, 37, 44,
    62, 63
Church Missionary Society, 44
City Hall (Lagos), 80
Civil war, *6,* 7, 8, 24, 25, *25,*
    43, 44, *44*
Climate, 15
Clothing, 81, *82*
Coal, 51, 69
Coastline, 9
Cocoa, 36, 53, 71, *72*
Columbite, 52, 70
Communication, 77
Composers, 66
Compounds, 58, 83
Constitutions, 39, 40, 41, 46,
    47
Cooperatives, 60

Courts, 47
Crafts, 22, 23, *23, 29, 34,* 74,
    75, 83
Crops, 24, 36, 53, 70, 71, *72*
Cross River, 14, 75
Crowther, Samuel Adjai, 37

Dams, *14,* 15
Dance, *16, 65,* 85
Darfur (Sudan), 32
Death rate, 60
Dimka, Musa, 46
Dodan, 46
Durbar, 40
Dutch (people), 35

East Central State, 7, 8
Eastern Highlands, 11
Eastern Region, 43
Edo (people), 57
Education, *46,* 47, 49
Edweme, Lazarus, 66
Efik (people), 35
Egungun festivals, 23, 83
Egypt, 31
Ekwensi, Cyprian, 68
Elizabeth II, 40
Elmina (Ghana), 35
Emirs, 27, 38, *38,* 86, 90
Emokapae, Erhabor, 67
Enugu, 43, 51, 52, 75, 76

Enwonwu, Ben, 67
Episcopalian church, 26
Esusu, 60
Ethnic groups, 18, 21, 22, 23, 24, 25, 26, *27*, 30, 31, 32, *32*, 33, 34, *34*, 35, 37, 39, 40, 43, 44, 46, 52, 57, 60, 62, 63, 64, 74, 75, 78, 81, 83, 84, *84*, 85, *88*, 89
Euba, Akin, 66
Explorers, 35, 36

Fakeye, Lamidi, 66
Farming, 24, 36, 53, 70, 71, *72*
Federal Executive Council, 47
Federal Institute of Industrial Research, 71
Federal Military Government (FMG), 43, 44, 47
Festivals, 23, *28*, 67, 83, 90
Fishing, *10*, *54*, 55, 71
Forests, 53
Fort Lamy (N'Djamena, Chad), 30
France (people), 35
Fulani (people), 25, 26, *27*, 30, 32, 33, 46, 57, 63, 64, *88*

Game reserves, 55, 85
Garba, Namvan, 45
Garoua (Cameroon), 75
"Getting up," 26, 60
Ghana, 35, 38, 45
Goldie, Sir George, 36
Gongola River, 14, 52, 75
Government, 38, 39, 40, 41, 46, 47
Gowon, Yakubu (Jack), 7, 21, 24, 43, 44, 45
Gowon, Yohanna, 44
Grains, 71
Groundnuts, 71, *72*, 87, *87*
Guinea, Gulf of, 9, 14, 71

Halawa, 28
Hausa (kingdoms), 32, 33, 35
Hausa (language), 33, 57, 85
Hausa (people), 25, 26, *32*, 33, 46, 52, 57, 63, 74, 84, 89
Hausa-Fulani (people), 26, 33, 46, 63
Health, 60, 61, 62
Herbalists, 62
Highlife, 66
Housing, 58, *59*, 83

Ibadan (city), 18, 22, 23, 49, 53, *53*, 58, 81, *82*, 83
Ibadan (state), 35

Ibadan, University of, 18, 22, 49, 81
Ibibio (people), 57, 62
Ibo (dynasty), 35
Ibo (people), 7, 8, 24, 25, 26, 37, 39, 40, 43, 57, 60, 62, 63, *89*
Iddo, 22, 79, 80
Ife, 22, 34, 49, 66, 83
Ife, University of, 22, 49
Ijaw (dynasty), 35
Ijaw (people), 57
Ijobu (state), 35
Ikoyi, 22, 79
Ile-Ife, 83
Ilorin, 49
Improvement Unions, 25, 60
Independence, 41
Indirect rule, 38
Industry, 74
Initiation rite, 30, 64
Insects, 55
International Festival of Black Arts and Culture, 23, 67
Iron, 52
Islam, 23, 25, *27*, 28, 32, 37, 47, 62, 63, 86

Jebba, 15
Jihad, 32
Jos, 17, 18, 49, 84, 85
Jos Plateau, 12, 14, 15, 18
Juju, 22, 80

Kaduna, 90
Kaduna River, 14
Kainji, 15
Kainji Dam, *14*, 15
Kainji Lake, 15, 55
Kaleri (people), 21, 84, *84*, 85
Kanem (Chad), 32
Kanem-Borno, 31, 32
Kano, 23, 26, 27, 28, 32, 33, *33*, 49, 75, 76, 85, 86, *86*, 87, 90
Kanuri (people), 57
Katsina, 32, 90
Katsina Ala River, 75
King's College, 47, 49
Kjaiye, 35
Koko, 83
Kola nuts, 28
Komadugu-Yobe River, 14
Koran, 27, 47, 62
Kurra waterfall, 85

Lagos, *20*, 21-24, 37, 38, 40, 41, 43, 44, 47, 58, 67, 71, 75, 76, 77, *78*, 79-81, *81*, *88*

Lagos Daily News, 39
Lagos Lagoon, *10*
Lagos, University of, 49
Laird, Macgregor, 36
Lakes, 12, 14, 15, 71
Languages, 19, 21, 26, 33, 49, 57, 68, 85
Life expectancy, 61
Lineage, 58, 63
Lingua franca, 33, 58
Literacy rate, 47
Literature, 68
Livestock, 71
Lokoja, 11, 38, 52
Lugard, Frederick, 38

Macauley, Herbert, 39, 40
Macpherson Constitution, 40
Maiduguri, 25, 49, 90
Mai Idris, 32
Makama Madawaki town house, 90
Mali, 31, 85
Mallam, 62
Mama (people), 18
Mangroves, 11, 53
Manufacturing, 74
Maps, 9, 13, 17, 48
Marketplaces, 22, 28, *67*, 74, *74*, 80, *82*, 83, 87
Marriage, 63, 64
Mecca (Saudi Arabia), 27, 28, 62
Miango, 85
Mid-Western Region, 41
Minerals and mining, 18, 51, 52, 69, 70
Mohammed, Murtala Ramat, 45, 46
Monogamy, 63
Mosques, 27, *28*, 86
Mountains, 11
Muhammad, Prophet, 62
Munoye, Jon, 68
Museums, 18, 21, 80, 83, 85, 90
Music, 22, 64, *65*, 66
Muslims, 23, 25, 27, 28, 32, 47, 62, 63, 86

National Development Plan, Second, 60
National Hall (Lagos), 80
Nationalism, 39, 40
National Universities Commission, 21
N'Djamena (Chad), 30
Niger, 11, 14, 15, 26, 76, 86
Niger-Benue valley, 11

Niger Coast Protectorate, 38
Nigeria Museum, Lagos, 21, 80
Nigerian National Democratic Party, 40
Nigerian Ports Authority, 75
Nigerian Society of Professional Artists, 66-67
Nigerian Youth Movement, 40
Nigeria, University of, 49
Niger River, 11, 12, 14, 15, 18, 36, 51, 54, 71, 75, 76
Niger valley, 11
Nok, 18, 85
Nok (people), 18, 31, 85
North Central state, 90
Northern High Plains, 12
Northern Region, 43, 49
North Western state, 90
Nsukka, 49
Nwapa, Flora, 68
Nxebwu, Onuora, 68

Obasanjo, Olasegun, 46
Obudu Uplands, 11
Ofala festival, 83
Oil, 51, *52*, 69, *70*
Oil Rivers Protectorate, 38
Ojukwu, E.O., 43, 44, 45
Ojukwu, Odumegwu, 8
Okeke, Uche, 67
Old Calabar, 35, 38
"Old People," 18, 84
Oloibiri, 51
Oni, 22
Onitsha, 7, 77, 83
Organization of African Unity, 44, 45
Osawe, Ben, 67
Osemwegie, Ikponmwosa, 68
Oshogbo, 23, 67, 83
Oshun, 23, 83
Ostriches, 55
Owerri, 7, 24-26
Oyelami, Muraina, 67
Oyo (kingdom), 34
Oyo (people), 22, 83

Palm oil, 36, *50*, 53, 71, 72
Palm trees, *50*, 53, 71, *72*
Park, Mungo, 36
Peanuts, 71, *72*, 87, *87*
Petroleum, 51, *52*, 69, *70*
Pisa, 18
Plateau state, 62
Polo, 29
Polygamy, 63
Population, 57
Port Harcourt, 43, 49, 75, 76
Ports, 75

Portuguese (people), 34, 35, 47
Prehistory, 31
Premier Hotel, 83

Railroads, 75, 76
Rainfall, 15
Ramadan, 23, 28, 62, 90
Religion, 23, 26, 36, 37, *37*, 44, 62, 63, 83
Richards Constitution, 40
Rivers, 11, 12, 14, 15, 18, 36, 51, 54, 71, 75, 76, 83
Roads, 76, *76*
Rowan, Carl, 7
Royal Niger Company, 36, 37, 38
Royal West African Frontier Force, 39
Rubber, 71, *73*
Rumfa, Muhammadu, 86

Sabon gari, 25, 90
Schools, 27, 47, 49
Sculpture, 66, *66*, 67
Seasons, 15
Sharo, 30, 64
Shebshi Hills, 11

Sierra Leone, 37
Slavery, 35
Soccer, 22
Social Welfare Division, 60
Sokinka, Wole, 22, 83
Sokoto (city), 49, 90
Sokoto Caliphate, 32, 33
Sokoto Plains, 12
Sokoto (state), 52
Sokoto River, 14
Songhai empire, 33
Southeastern Lowlands, 12
Southeastern Scarplands, 12
Soviet Union, 52
Sowande, Fela, 66
Soy-ogi, 71
"Special friend," 64
Sports, 22, 29
States, 43, 44, 47
Subsistence farming, 71
Sudan, 31, 32
Supreme Military Council, 47
Suspension and Modification Decree, 47
Swamps, 11, 53

Tarkwa Beach, 21, 79

Temperatures, 15
Timbuktu (Mali), 31, 33, 85
Tin, 18, 51, 52, 70, 85
Tinubu, Madame, 36
Tiv (people), 18, 57, 85
Togo, 76
Transportation, 75, 76, *76*, 77
Trees, *50*, 53
Tutuola, Amos, 68
Twins Seven Seven, 67

United Africa Company, 36
United States of America, 18, 69
Universities, 18, 21, 22, 49, 81, 90
University College, 49
Utuman (Usuman) Dan Fodio, 32, 33

Victoria (Queen of England), 37
Victoria (island), 79
Victorian Beach, *80*
Vogel Peak, 11

Warri, 75

Waterfalls, 85
Wazirci Ward Primary School, 27
Wenger, Suzanne, 83
West African School Certificate, 49
Western High Plains, 11
Western Region, 41, 43
"White man's graveyard," 15
Women, 26, 30, 60, 83
World War I, 39
World War II, 40
Writers, 22, 68, 83

Yankari Game Reserve, 55, 85
Yelwa, 75
Yemen, 31
Yola, 75
Yoruba (people), 21, 22, 23, 34, *34*, 37, 39, 40, 57, 60, 62, 63, 75, 81, 83, 84

Zaria, 49, 90
Zazzau Emirate, 90
Zurak, 52

About the Author

With the publication of his first book for school use when he was twenty, **Allan Carpenter** began a career as an author that has spanned more than 135 books—with more still to be published in the Enchantment of Africa series for Childrens Press. After teaching in the public schools of Des Moines, Mr. Carpenter began his career as an educational publisher at the age of twenty-one when he founded the magazine *Teachers Digest.* In the field of educational periodicals, he was responsible for many innovations. During his many years in publishing, he has perfected a highly organized approach to handling large volumes of factual material: after extensive traveling and having collected all possible materials, he systematically reviews and organizes everything. From his apartment high in Chicago's John Hancock Building, Allan recalls: "My collection and assimilation of materials on the states and countries began before the publication of my first book." Allan is the founder of Carpenter Publishing House and of Infordata International, Inc., publishers of *Issues in Education* and *Index to U.S. Government Periodicals.* When he is not writing or traveling, his principal avocation is music. He has been the principal bassist of many symphonies, and he managed the country's leading non-professional symphony for twenty-five years.

729-4851